Pearl of Wisdom

Buddhist Prayers & Practices

Book II

Pearl of Wisdom

Buddhist Prayers & Practices

Book II

Compiled by Bhikshuni Thubten Chodron

First edition 1988
Sixth edition (revised) 2014

For further information contact:
Sravasti Abbey
    692 Country Lane
    Newport, WA 99156, USA
    Email: office.sravasti@gmail.com
    http://www.sravasti.org

For audio and video Dharma talks see:
    http://www.thubtenchodron.org
    http://www.youtube.com/sravastiabbey
    http://sravasti.org/programs/internet.html

To hear melodies for chanting verses and mantras go to:
    http://www.thubtenchodron.org/PrayersandPractices/index

Books by Ven. Thubten Chodron:
    An Open-hearted Life: Transformative Methods for Compassionate Living from a Clinical Psychologist and a Buddhist Nun (co-authored with Dr. Russell Kolts, Snow Lion Publications*)*
    Buddhism for Beginners (Snow Lion Publications)
    Buddhism: One Teacher, Many Traditions (co-authored with His Holiness the 14th Dalai Lama, Wisdom Publications*)*
    Cultivating a Compassionate Heart: The Yoga Method of Chenrezig (Snow Lion Publications)
    Guided Meditations on the Stages of the Path (Snow Lion Publications)
    How to Free Your Mind: Tara the Liberator (Snow Lion Publications)
    Open Heart, Clear Mind (Snow Lion Publications)
    The Path to Happiness (Texas Buddhist Association)
    Taming the Mind (Snow Lion Publications)
    Working with Anger (Snow Lion Publications)

© Sravasti Abbey 2014
ISBN 978-0-9858498-2-5
Cover design by Ven. Thubten Jigme

Table of Contents

Introduction vi

Meditation on 1000-Armed Chenrezig 1

Meditation on Arya Tara 10

Lama Tsongkhapa Guru Yoga 24

Vajrasattva Purification 37

Medicine Buddha Meditation 43

White Tara Meditation 48

Meditation on Amitabha Buddha 51

Prayer to Be Reborn in the Land of Bliss 58

The King of Prayers 64

Aspiring and Engaging Bodhicitta 73

Various Mantras 84

Scriptural Quotations for Meditation 87

Notes 95

Introduction

Pearl of Wisdom Book I is designed for those embarking on Dharma practice. This book, *Book II*, is for people who have already entered into practice. Although some of the practices contained here are deity practices, people who have not yet received empowerment may do them. However, it is advisable to do them under the instruction of a teacher. If you simply pick up this book to "try it out for yourself," you will not understand the practices and their purpose.

Guidance from a teacher is essential to help you understand what qualities the prayers and practices are designed to develop and how to think while doing the recitations. Instruction from a teacher is especially helpful to know how to do the visualization technique properly. Also, receiving explanation on the prayers and practices clarifies the meaning of unfamiliar terms and concepts.

These prayers and practices are very effective for purifying past destructive actions and for building up a store of merit. To receive full benefit from these practices, it is good to integrate them with analytical meditation on the stages of the path to awakening. (Detailed instruction for doing these can be found in my book, *Guided Meditations on the Stages of the Path*, published by Snow Lion.)

For example, when you do the meditation on 1000-Armed Chenrezig, before dedicating the merit, insert a brief analytical meditation on one of the topics in the stages of the path. In this way, you will purify negativities, accumulate merit, strengthen your connection to Chenrezig, and increase your understanding and experience of the stages of the path to awakening all in one meditation session.

To this edition we have added three practices that are good to recite to help the deceased: the Meditation on Amitabha Buddha, "Prayer to Be Reborn in the Land of Bliss," and "The King of Prayers." For people who are ill, doing the practices of Medicine Buddha, White Tara, and Amitabha Buddha are helpful. The Chenrezig Meditation is especially inspiring when you want to awaken compassion, and the Meditation on Arya Tara is helpful when facing obstacles and difficulties. Doing the Lama Tsongkhapa Guru Yoga before engaging in Dharma study will increase wisdom and enhance your ability to understand. Of course, reciting the prayers and practicing the meditations benefit and inspire us at other times as well!

More information on the Chenrezig practice can be found in my book, *Cultivating a Compassionate Heart: The Yoga Method of Chenrezig*. *How to Free Your Mind: The Practice of Tara the Liberator* contains instruction on the Tara practice.

Zopa Rinpoche compiled the Chenrezig and Vajrasattva meditations in this book. Geshe Jampa Gyatso helped with the section on aspiring and engaging bodhicitta, and Jesse Fenton did the translation of "The Extraordinary Aspiration of the Practice of Samantabhadra." Any errors are mine.

Bhikshuni Thubten Chodron
Sravasti Abbey, 2014

Meditation on 1000-Armed Chenrezig

Visualization

In the space in front of me is the divine form of 1000-Armed Chenrezig, who is the embodiment of all the infinite Buddhas' compassionate wisdom. He stands on a lotus and moon seat. His body is in the nature of white light, youthful, and decorated with magnificent jeweled ornaments.

He has eleven faces. Of the three on his shoulders, his center face is white, the right green, and the left red. Above those, his center face is green, right red, and left white. Above those, his center face is red, right white, and left green. Above those is a wrathful dark blue face with yellow hair standing erect. On top of that is the red head of Amitabha Buddha, peaceful and smiling.

Chenrezig's first two hands are at his heart, palms together, holding a wish-fulfilling gem. On his right, the second hand holds a crystal rosary, reminding me to recite the mantra. The third hand is in the gesture of giving realizations, and from it a rain of nectar falls, curing the hunger and thirst of the hungry ghosts. The fourth hand holds a Dharma wheel.

On his left, the second hand holds a white lotus, the purest of flowers, although it is born from the mud. The third hand holds a vase containing the nectar of his compassionate wisdom. The fourth holds a bow and arrow, symbolizing defeat of the four negative forces. The other 992 hands are in the gesture of giving the highest realizations. An antelope skin is draped over his left shoulder, symbolizing that hatred is overcome completely by peaceful, compassionate wisdom.

2   MEDITATION ON 1000-ARMED CHENREZIG

Taking Refuge and Generating the Altruistic Intention (Bodhicitta)

I take refuge until I have awakened in the Buddha, the Dharma and the Sangha. By the merit I create by engaging in generosity and the other far-reaching practices, may I attain Buddhahood in order to benefit all sentient beings. (Recite 3 times from the depth of your heart.)

The Four Immeasurables

How wonderful it would be if all sentient beings were to abide in equanimity, free of bias, attachment, and anger. May they abide in this way. I shall cause them to abide in this way. Guru Chenrezig, please inspire me to be able to do so.

How wonderful it would be if all sentient beings had happiness and its causes. May they have these. I shall cause them to have these. Guru Chenrezig, please inspire me to be able to do so.

How wonderful it would be if all sentient beings were free from suffering and its causes. May they be free. I shall cause them to be free. Guru Chenrezig, please inspire me to be able to do so.

How wonderful it would be if all sentient beings were never parted from upper rebirth and liberation's excellent bliss. May they never be parted. I shall cause them never to be parted. Guru Chenrezig, please inspire me to be able to do so.

Seven-Limb Prayer

Reverently I prostrate with my body, speech, and mind,
And present clouds of every type of offering, actual and mentally
transformed.
I confess all my destructive actions accumulated since
beginningless time,
And rejoice in the virtues of all holy and ordinary beings.
Please remain until cyclic existence ends,
And turn the wheel of Dharma for sentient beings.
I dedicate all the virtues of myself and others to the great
awakening.

Mandala Offering

This ground, anointed with perfume, flowers strewn,
Mount Meru, four lands, sun and moon,
Imagined as a Buddha land and offered to you.
May all beings enjoy this pure land.

The objects of attachment, aversion, and ignorance—friends,
enemies, and strangers, my body, wealth, and enjoyments—I offer
these without any sense of loss. Please accept them with pleasure,
and inspire me and others to be free from the three poisonous
attitudes.

Idam guru ratna mandalakam nirya tayami

4　MEDITATION ON 1000-ARMED CHENREZIG

Request Prayer

O Arya, Compassionate-eyed One,
Who is the treasure of compassion,
I request you, please listen to me.
Please guide myself, mothers, and fathers
In all six realms to be freed quickly
From the great ocean of samsara.
I request that the vast and profound
Peerless awakening mind may grow.
With the tear of your great compassion,
Please cleanse all karmas and delusion.
Please lead with your hand of compassion
Me and migrators to fields of bliss.
Please Amitabha and Chenrezig,
In all my lives be virtuous friends.
Show well the undeceptive pure path,
And quickly place us in Buddha's state.

Meditation on the "Eight Verses of Thought Transformation"

(Contemplate each verse as you read it and apply it to your life.)

1.   With the thought of attaining awakening
    For the welfare of all beings,
    Who are more precious than a wish-fulfilling jewel,
    I will constantly practice holding them dear.

2.   Whenever I am with others
    I will practice seeing myself as the lowest of all,
    And from the very depth of my heart,
    I will respectfully hold others as supreme.

3. In all actions I will examine my mind,
   And the moment a disturbing attitude arises,
   Endangering myself and others,
   I will firmly confront and avert it.

4. Whenever I meet a person of bad nature,
   Who is overwhelmed by negative energy and intense
   suffering,
   I will hold such a rare one dear,
   As if I had found a precious treasure.

5. When others, out of jealousy,
   Mistreat me with abuse, slander, and so on,
   I will practice accepting defeat
   And offering the victory to them.

6. When someone I have benefited
   And in whom I have placed great trust
   Hurts me very badly,
   I will practice seeing that person as my supreme teacher.

7. In short, I will offer directly and indirectly
   Every benefit and happiness to all beings, my mothers.
   I will practice in secret taking upon myself
   All their harmful actions and sufferings.

8. Without these practices being defiled by the stains of the
   eight worldly concerns,
   By perceiving all phenomena as illusory,
   I will practice without grasping to release all beings
   From the bondage of the disturbing unsubdued mind and
   karma.

6   MEDITATION ON 1000-ARMED CHENREZIG

Purification and Receiving Inspiration

Chenrezig now comes on top of your head, facing the same direction as you. Chenrezig also appears on the heads of all sentient beings who are seated around you. At the heart of each Chenrezig are a lotus and flat moon disc. Standing at the center of the moon is the seed-syllable HRI, the essence of Chenrezig's omniscient mind of wisdom and compassion. This is surrounded by the letters of the long mantra, and inside this stand the letters of the six-syllable mantra. All is made of radiant light.

From the mantras and HRI, much white light and nectar, the nature of Chenrezig's blissful omniscient mind, flow into you, permeating your entire nervous system. They totally purify all afflictions, imprints of negative karma, diseases, and obscurations. Feel completely pure and blissful. The light and nectar also fill you with all the realizations of the stages of the path to awakening, especially Chenrezig's love, compassion, and wisdom.

Similarly, light and nectar from the Chenrezigs on the crowns of all the sentient beings flow into them, purifying all negativities and obscurations and inspiring them with all the realizations of the path to awakening. (Do this visualization while reciting the long mantra and then the six-syllable mantra.)

Long mantra:

namo ratna trayaya/ namo arya gyana sagara/ berotsana buha radzaya/ tatagataya/ arhate/ samyaksam buddhaya/ namo sarwa tatagatebhye/ arhatebhye/ samyaksam buddhebhye/ namo arya awalokite/ shoraya/ bodhi satoya/ maha satoya/ maha karunikaya/ tayata om/ dara dara/ diri diri/ duru duru/ itte wate/ tsale tsale/ partsale partsale/ kusume kusume ware/ ihli mili/ tsiti dzola/ ahpanaye soha/

Six-syllable mantra:

om mani padme hum

Absorption

Think: "I will live my life in a meaningful way and do all actions with the motivation to attain awakening for the benefit of all sentient beings." Because you have such a noble intention, Chenrezig is extremely pleased. He melts into white light and absorbs into your heart.

By Chenrezig absorbing into you, your mind becomes the nature of great compassion, loving-kindness, and bodhicitta. Your body is filled with light and becomes very pure and clear, like crystal. Concentrate on this for a while.

The Chenrezigs on the heads of all the sentient beings melt into light, absorb into them, and inspire them so that they may progress along the stages of the path to awakening.

Dedication

Due to this merit may we soon
Attain the awakened state of Chenrezig
That we may be able to liberate
All sentient beings from their sufferings.

May the precious bodhi mind
Not yet born arise and grow.
May that born have no decline
But increase forever more.

Due to the merit accumulated by myself and others in the past, present, and future, may anyone who merely sees, hears, remembers, touches, or talks to me be freed in that very instant from all sufferings and abide in happiness forever.

In all rebirths, may I and all sentient beings be born in a good family, have clear wisdom and great compassion, be free of pride and devoted to our spiritual mentors, and abide within the vows and commitments to our spiritual mentors.

In whatever guise you appear, O Chenrezig, whatever your retinue, your life span and pure land, whatever your name most noble and holy, may I and all others attain only these.

By the force of these praises and requests made to you, may all disease, poverty, fighting, and quarrels be calmed. May the Dharma and all auspiciousness increase throughout the worlds and directions where I and all others dwell.

Daily Activities

When doing your daily activities, visualize and be mindful of a small Chenrezig made of radiant light at your heart or on top of your head. Thinking that Chenrezig is a witness to all you do or say will increase your mindfulness and compassion for others. When you eat or enjoy other sense pleasures, imagine offering them to Chenrezig. Whenever you are praised, rather than get arrogant, think Chenrezig is being praised.

Request to the Supreme Compassionate One

Namo Guru Lokeshvaraya.

Praise to the beautiful Four-Armed Lord of the World, supreme embodiment of all the three-time conquerors, possessing supremacy, excellent holder of the lotus. Your stainless feet beautifully adorn my crown.

May the karmic pollution of myself and others be washed away by your cool compassionate tear, great loving protector, sole refuge of pitiful, guideless migrating beings, you who first generated bodhicitta and then reached culmination.

O merciful one, please behold with your compassionate eye the beings of unfortunate rebirths, caught in realms difficult to escape, experiencing individual results of destructive actions as hell beings, hungry ghosts, animals, demi-gods, and the rest.

Behold with compassion the thoughtless ones who return empty-handed; even their high rebirths were without meaning. Their human bodies were so rare and fragile, but their lives were consumed only in suffering. Amidst their endless actions, the Lord of Death arrived.

Behold with compassion tough-skinned beings like me, who maintain a religious manner but do not achieve the great meaning, being overwhelmed by attachment, hatred and the eight worldly concerns, without having subdued our minds by observing cause and effect.

With compassion please lead those without refuge on the path; for when the vision of this life fades, the vision of their self-created karma arises as the enemy in the intermediate state, and they are taken on a precipitous route by Yama's messenger.

Look upon us with compassion, Guru Avalokiteshvara, mother attached by compassion to all sentient beings, who is the special, sole refuge of the Land of Snows. May I and all others quickly attain your state of awakening.

Meditation on Arya Tara

Refuge and Bodhicitta

I take refuge until I have awakened in the Buddha, the Dharma, and the Sangha. By the merit I create by engaging in generosity and the other far-reaching practices, may I attain Buddhahood in order to benefit all sentient beings. (3x)

The Four Immeasurables

May all sentient beings have happiness and its causes.
May all sentient beings be free of suffering and its causes.
May all sentient beings not be separated from sorrowless bliss.
May all sentient beings abide in equanimity, free of bias, attachment, and anger.

The Actual Practice

In the space above, on a lotus and moon seat, sits Arya Tara, emerald green, with one face and two arms. Her right hand is in the gesture of supreme giving, fulfilling the wishes of all beings. Her left hand is at her heart in the gesture of the Three Jewels. Always present to liberate living beings, but never affected by the defects of cyclic existence, she holds blue utpala flowers.

She is extremely beautiful, representing all goodness in visible form, adorned with jeweled ornaments and heavenly silks. To symbolize the union of method and wisdom, she sits with her right leg slightly extended and her left bent. On her crown is Amitabha Buddha. Tara sits amidst an aura of light, her three places adorned with three vajras—OM at her crown, AH at her throat, HUM at her heart.

MEDITATION ON ARYA TARA   11

Surrounding her in space are the 21 Taras, as well as all Buddhas and bodhisattvas. Surrounding you are all sentient beings. Imagine leading them in reciting the prayers and requests to Tara.

Seven-Limb Prayer

Reverently I prostrate with my body, speech, and mind,
And present clouds of every type of offering, actual and mentally transformed.
I confess all my destructive actions accumulated since beginningless time,
And rejoice in the virtues of all holy and ordinary beings.
Please remain until cyclic existence ends,
And turn the wheel of Dharma for sentient beings.
I dedicate the virtues created by myself and others to the great awakening.

Mandala Offering

This ground, anointed with perfume, flowers strewn,
Mount Meru, four lands, sun and moon,
Imagined as a Buddha land and offered to you.
May all beings enjoy this pure land.

The objects of attachment, aversion, and ignorance—friends, enemies, and strangers, my body, wealth, and enjoyments—I offer these without any sense of loss. Please accept them with pleasure, and inspire me and others to be free from the three poisonous attitudes.

Idam guru ratna mandalakam nirya tayami

12   MEDITATION ON ARYA TARA

Homage to the Twenty-one Taras (Tibetan)

OM je tsun ma pag ma dro ma la chag tsel lo

1. Chag tsel drol ma nyur ma pa mo
    Chen ni kay chig log dang dra ma
    Jig ten sum gom chu kye zhel gyi
    Ge sar je wa lay ni jung ma

2. Chag tsel ton kay da wa kun tu
    Gang wa gya ni tseg pay zhel ma
    Kar ma tong trag tsog pa nam kyi
    Rab tu che way o rab bar ma

3. Chag tsel ser ngo chu nay kye kyi
    Pay may chag ni nam par gyen ma
    Jin pa tsun du ka tub shi wa
    So pa sam ten cho yul nyi ma

4. Chag tsel de shin sheg pay tsug tor
    Ta yay nam par gyel wa cho ma
    Ma lu pa rol chin pa tob pay
    Gyel way say kyi shin tu ten ma

5. Chag tsel tu ta ra hum yi ge
    Do dang chog dang nam ka gang ma
    Jig ten dun po shab kyi nen te
    Lu pa me par gug par nu ma

6. Chag tsel gya jin may lha tsang pa
    Lung lha na tsog wang chug cho ma
    Jung po ro lang dri za nam dang
    No jin tsog kyi dun nay to ma

7. Chag tsel trey che cha dang pay kyi
    Pa rol tul kor rab tu jom ma
    Yay kum yon kyang shab kyi nen te
    May bar tug pa shin tu bar ma

MEDITATION ON ARYA TARA   13

Homage to the Twenty-one Taras

OM I prostrate to the noble transcendent liberator.

1. Homage to Tara swift and fearless,
   With eyes like a flash of lightning,
   Lotus-born in an ocean of tears
   Of Chenrezig, three worlds' protector.

2. Homage to you whose face is like
   One hundred autumn moons gathered
   And blazes with the dazzling light
   Of a thousand constellations.

3. Homage to you born from a gold-blue lotus
   Hands adorned with lotus flowers,
   Essence of giving, effort, and ethics,
   Fortitude, concentration, and wisdom.

4. Homage to you who crown all Buddhas,
   Whose action subdues without limit.
   Attained to every perfection,
   On you the bodhisattvas rely.

5. Homage to you whose *tuttare* and *hum*
   Fill the realms of desire, form and space.
   You crush seven worlds beneath your feet
   And have power to call all forces.

6. Homage to you adored by Indra,
   Agni, Brahma, Vayu, and Ishvara,
   Praised in song by hosts of spirits,
   Zombies, scent-eaters, and yakshas.

7. Homage to you whose *trey* and *pey*
   Destroy external wheels of magic.
   Right leg drawn in and left extended,
   You blaze within a raging fire.

14   MEDITATION ON ARYA TARA

8. Chag tsel tu re jig pa chen po
    Du kyi pa wo nam par jom ma
    Chu kye shel ni tro nyer den dze
    Dra wo tam chay ma lu so ma

9. Chag tsel kon chog sum tson chag gyay
    Sor mo tug kar nam par gyen ma
    Ma lu chog kyi kor lo gyen pay
    Rang gi o kyi tsog nam tug ma

10. Chag tsel rab tu ga wa ji pay
    U gyen o kyi treng wa pel ma
    Shay pa rab shay tu ta ra yi
    Du dang jig ten wang du dze ma

11. Chag tsel sa shi kyong way tsog nam
    Tam chay gug par nu ma nyi ma
    Tro nyer yo way yi ge hum ki
    Pong pa tam chay nam par dol ma

12. Chag tsel da way dum bu u gyen
    Gyen pa tam chay shin tu bar ma
    Rel pay tro na o pag may lay
    Tag par shin tu o rab dze ma

13. Chag tsel kel pay ta may may tar
    Bar way treng way u na nay ma
    Yay kang yon kum kun nay kor gay
    Dra yi pung ni nam par jom ma

14. Chag tsel sa shi ngo la chag gi
    Til gyi nun ching zhab gyi dung ma
    Tro nyer chen dze yi gay hum ki
    Rim pa dun po nam ni ghem ma

15. Chag tsel de ma gay ma zhi ma
    Nya ngen day zhi cho yul nyi ma
    So ha om dang yang dag den pay
    Dig pa chen po jom pa nyi ma

MEDITATION ON ARYA TARA   15

8. Homage to you whose *ture* destroys
    The great fears, the mighty demons.
    With a wrathful frown on your lotus face,
    You slay all foes without exception.

9. Homage to you beautifully adorned
    By the Three Jewels' gesture at your heart.
    Your wheel shines in all directions
    With a whirling mass of light.

10. Homage to you, radiant and joyful,
    Whose crown emits a garland of light.
    You, by the laughter of *tuttara,*
    Conquer demons and lords of the world.

11. Homage to you with power to invoke
    The assembly of local protectors.
    With your fierce frown and vibrating *hum,*
    You bring freedom from all poverty.

12. Homage to you with crescent moon crown,
    All your adornments dazzling bright.
    From your hair knot, Amitabha
    Shines eternal with great beams of light.

13. Homage to you who dwells in a blazing wreath
    Like the fire at the end of this age.
    Your right leg outstretched and left drawn in,
    Joy surrounds you who defeats hosts of foes.

14. Homage to you whose foot stamps the earth
    And whose palm strikes the ground by your side.
    With a wrathful glance and the letter *hum,*
    You subdue all in the seven stages.

15. Homage to the blissful, virtuous, peaceful one,
    Object of practice, nirvana's peace,
    Perfectly endowed with *soha* and *om,*
    Overcoming all the great evils.

16 MEDITATION ON ARYA TARA

16. Chag tsel kun nay kor rab ga way
Dra ye lu ni nam par ghem ma
Yig gay chu pay ngag ni ko pay
Rig pa hum lay dol ma nyi ma

17. Chag tsel tu re zab ni dab pay
Hum gi nam pay sa bon nyi ma
Ri rab man da ra dang big je
Jig ten sum nam yo wa nyi ma

18. Chag tsel lha yi tso yi nam pay
Ri dag tag chen chag na nam ma
Ta ra nyi jo pey kyi yi gay
Dug nam ma lu pa ni sel ma

19. Chag tsel lha yi tsog nam gyel po
Lha dang mi am chi yi ten ma
Kun nay go cha ga way ji kyi
Tso dang mi lam nyen pa sel ma

20. Chag tsel nyi ma da wa gyay pay
Chen nyi po la o rab sel ma
Ha ra nyi jo tu ta ra yi
Shin tu dag po rim nay sel ma

21. Chag tsel de nyi sum nam ko pay
Zi way tu dang yang dag den ma
Don dang ro lang no jin tsog nam
Jom pa tu re rab chog nyi ma

Tsa way ngag kyi to pa di dang
Chag tsel wa ni nyi shu tsa chig /

16. Homage to you with joyous retinue;
    You subdue fully all enemies' forms.
    The ten-letter mantra adorns your heart,
    And your knowledge—*hum*—gives liberation.

17. Homage to *ture* with stamping feet,
    Whose essence is the seed-letter *hum*.
    You cause Meru, Mandara, and Vindya,
    And all three worlds to tremble and shake.

18. Homage to you who holds in your hand
    A moon like a celestial lake.
    Saying *tara* twice and the letter *pey*,
    You dispel all poisons without exception.

19. Homage to you on whom the kings of gods,
    The gods themselves, and all spirits rely.
    Your armor radiates joy to all.
    You soothe conflicts and nightmares as well.

20. Homage to you whose eyes, the sun and moon,
    Radiate with pure brilliant light.
    Uttering *hara* twice and *tuttara*
    Dispels extremely fearful plagues.

21. Homage to you, adorned with three natures,
    Perfectly endowed with peaceful strength.
    You destroy demons, zombies, and yakshas.
    O Ture, most exalted and sublime!

    Thus the root mantra is praised,
    And twenty-one homages offered.

18 MEDITATION ON ARYA TARA

MEDITATION ON ARYA TARA   19

The Condensed Praise

OM to the transcendent subduer, Arya Tara, I prostrate.
Homage to the glorious one who frees with TARE;
With TUTTARA you calm all fears;
You bestow all success with TURE;
To the sound SOHA I pay great homage.

Requesting Protection from the Eight Dangers
by the First Dalai Lama

Dwelling in the mountains of wrong views of selfhood,
Puffed up with holding itself superior,
It claws other beings with contempt,
The lion of conceit—please protect us from this danger!

Untamed by the sharp hooks of mindfulness and
introspective awareness,
Dulled by the maddening liquor of sensual pleasures,
It enters wrong paths and shows its harmful tusks,
The elephant of ignorance—please protect us from this danger!

Driven by the wind of inappropriate attention,
Billowing swirling smoke-clouds of misconduct,
It has the power to burn down forests of goodness,
The fire of anger—please protect us from this danger!

Lurking in its dark pit of ignorance,
Unable to bear the wealth and excellence of others,
It swiftly injects them with its cruel poison,
The snake of jealousy—please protect us from this danger!

20   MEDITATION ON ARYA TARA

Roaming the fearful wild of inferior practice
And the barren wastes of absolutism and nihilism,
They sack the towns and hermitages of benefit and bliss,
The thieves of wrong views—please protect us from this danger!

Binding embodied beings in the unbearable prison
Of cyclic existence with no freedom,
It locks them in craving's tight embrace,
The chain of miserliness—please protect us from this danger!

Sweeping us in the torrent of cyclic existence so hard to cross,
Where, conditioned by the propelling winds of karma,
We are tossed in the waves of birth, aging, sickness, and death,
The flood of attachment—please protect us from this danger!

Roaming in the space of darkest confusion,
Tormenting those who strive for ultimate aims,
It is viciously lethal to liberation,
The carnivorous demon of doubt—please protect us from
this danger!

Through these praises and requests to you,
Quell conditions unfavorable for Dharma practice,
And let us have long life, merit, glory, plenty,
And other conducive conditions as we wish!

Purification and Inspiration

Visualize much radiant and blissful green light from the TAM and
mantra syllables at Tara's heart streaming into you and into the
sentient beings surrounding you. This light purifies the imprints of
all destructive actions, pacifies all afflictions, fear, and anxiety,
and dispels all sickness and harms from negative forces. The light
brings inspiration and blessings from Tara, enabling you to realize

MEDITATION ON ARYA TARA   21

the stages of the path to awakening. While doing the visualization, recite Tara's peaceful mantra:

om tare tuttare ture soha

Because you have the attitude to not harm and to benefit others, Arya Tara is extremely pleased. She comes on top of your head, melts into green radiating light, and dissolves into you. Your body, speech, and mind become inseparable from Arya Tara's holy body, speech, and mind. Concentrate on this for as long as you can.

Lamrim Meditation

(Meditate on the Lamrim, the stages of the path to awakening. You may do this according to meditation outlines, or recite "The Three Principal Aspects of the Path" and meditate deeply on it.)

Dedication

Due to this merit may I soon
Attain the awakened state of Arya Tara.
That I may be able to liberate
All sentient beings from their suffering.

May the precious bodhi mind
Not yet born arise and grow.
May that born have no decline
But increase forever more.

Due to this merit, may the Venerable Lady Tara take care of me and all sentient beings. May we see the face of Amitabha Buddha in Sukhavati, and may we enjoy the Mahayana teachings.

22   MEDITATION ON ARYA TARA

O compassionate and venerable subduer, may the infinite beings, including myself soon purify the two obscurations and complete both collections so that we may attain full awakening.

For all of my lives, until I reach this stage, may I know the sublime happiness of humans and gods. So that I may become fully omniscient, please pacify quickly all obstacles, spirits, obstructions, epidemics, diseases, and so forth, the various causes of untimely death, bad dreams and omens, the eight dangers, and other afflictions, and make it so that they no longer exist.

May the mundane and supramundane collections of all excellent auspicious qualities and happiness increase and develop, and may all wishes be fulfilled naturally and effortlessly, without an exception.

May I strive to realize and increase the sacred Dharma, accomplishing your stage and beholding your sublime face. May my understanding of emptiness and the precious bodhicitta increase like the moon waxing full.

May I be reborn from an extremely beautiful and holy lotus in the joyous and noble mandala of the conqueror. May I attain whatever prophecy I receive in the presence of Amitabha Buddha.

O deity whom I have practiced in previous lives, the enlightening influence of the three-time Buddhas, emerald green with one face and two arms, the swift pacifier, O mother holding an utpala flower, may you be auspicious!

Whatever your body, O Mother of Conquerors, whatever your retinue, lifespan and pure land, whatever your name, most noble and holy, may I and all others attain only these.

By the force of these praises and requests made to you, may all disease, poverty, fighting, and quarrels be calmed. May the precious Dharma and everything auspicious increase throughout the world and directions where I and all others dwell.

Lama Tsongkhapa Guru Yoga
(Tibetan)

Refuge and generating the dedicated heart

sang gye cho dang tsog kyi cho nam la
jang chub bar du dag nyi kyab su chi
dag gi jin sog gi pay so nam kyi
dro la pen chir sang gye drub par shog

Actual practice

ga den lha gyi gon gyi tug ka nay
rab kar zho sar pung dri chu dzin tse
cho kyi gyal po kun kyen lo zang drag
say dang chay pa nay dir sheg su sol

dun gyi nam ka seng dri pay day teng
je tsun la ma gye pay dzum kar chen
dag lo day pay so nam zhing chog du
ten pa gye chir kal gyar zhug su sol

shay je kyon kun jal way lo dro tug
kal zang na way gyen gyur leg shay sung
drag pay pel gyi lham may dze pay ku
tong to dren pay don den la chag tsal

yi ong cho yon na tsog may tog dang
dri zhim dub po nang sel dri chab sog
ngo sham yi trul cho trin gya tso di
so nam zhing chog kyo la cho par bul

Lama Tsongkhapa Guru Yoga

Refuge and Bodhicitta

I take refuge until I have awakened in the Buddha, the Dharma and the Sangha. By the merit I create by engaging in generosity and the other far-reaching practices, may I attain Buddhahood in order to benefit all sentient beings. (3x)

Actual Practice: Visualization and offering the seven-limb prayer

From the heart of the Lord Protector of Tushita's hundred gods,
Floating on fluffy white clouds, piled up like fresh curd,
Comes the Omniscient Lord of the Dharma, Losang Dragpa.
Please come here, together with your spiritual heirs.[1]

In the sky before me, on a lion throne with lotus and moon seat,
Sits the holy guru with his beautiful smiling face.
Supreme field of merit for my mind of faith,
Please stay one hundred eons to spread the teachings.

Your mind of pure genius that spans the whole range
of knowledge,
Your speech of eloquence, jewel ornament for the fortunate ear,
Your body of beauty, resplendent with the glory of fame,
I bow to you so beneficial to see, hear, and remember.

Various delightful offerings of flowers, perfumes,
Incense, lights, and pure sweet waters, those actually presented
And this ocean of offering clouds created by my imagination,
I offer to you, O supreme field of merit.

dag gi tog may du nay sag pa yi
lu ngag yi kyi mi gay chi gyi dang
kye par dom pa sum gyi mi tun chog
nying nay kyo pa drag po so sor shag

nyig may du dir mang to drub la tson
cho gye pang pay dal jor don yu jay
gon po kyo kyi lab chen dze pa la
dag chag sam pa tag pay yi rang ngo

je tsun la ma dam pa kye nam kyi
cho ku ka la kyen tse chu dzin drig
ji tar tsam pay dul jay dzin ma la
zab gye cho kyi char pa ab tu sol

dag gi ji nye sag pay gay wa di
ten dang dro wa kun la gang pen dang
kye par je tsun lo zang drag pa yi
ten pay nying po ring du sel jay shog

Short Mandala Offering
sa zhi po kyi jug shing may tog tram
ri rab ling zhi nyi day gyan pa di
sang gye zhing du mig tay ul war gyi
dro kun nam dag zhing la cho par shog

idam guru ratna mandalakam nirya tayami

Short Request to Je Tsongkhapa
mig may tse way ter chen chen re sig
dri may kyen pay wong po jam pel yang
du pung ma lu jom dze sang way dag
gang chen kay pay tsug kyen tsong kha pa
lo zang drag pay zhab la sol wa deb

All the negativities I have committed with body, speech, and mind
Accumulated from beginningless time,
And especially all transgressions of the three ethical codes,
I confess each one with strong regret from the depth of my heart.

In this degenerate time, you worked for broad learning and accomplishment,
Abandoning the eight worldly concerns to realize the great value
Of freedom and fortune; sincerely, O Protector,
I rejoice at your great deeds.

Venerable holy Gurus, in the space of your truth body,
From billowing clouds of your wisdom and love,
Let fall the rain of the profound and extensive Dharma
In whatever form is suitable for subduing sentient beings.

Whatever virtue I may have gathered here,
May it bring benefit to the migrating beings and to the Buddha's teachings.
May it make the essence of Buddha's doctrine,
And especially the teachings of Venerable Losang Dragpa, shine for a long time.

Short Mandala Offering
This ground, anointed with perfume, flowers strewn,
Mount Meru, four lands, sun and moon,
Imagined as a Buddha land and offered to you.
May all beings enjoy this pure land.

idam guru ratna mandalakam nirya tayami

Short request to Je Tsongkhapa
Avalokiteshvara, great treasure of objectless compassion,
Manjushri, master of flawless wisdom,
Vajrapani, destroyer of all demonic forces,
Tsongkhapa, crown jewel of the Snowy Lands' sages
Losang Dragpa, I make request at your holy feet.

Nine-line request to Lama Tsongkhapa

ngo drup kun jung tub wang dor je chang
mig may tse way ter chen chen re sig
dri may kyen pay wong po jam pel yang
du pung ma lu jom dze sang way dag
gang chen kay pay tsug kyen lo zang drag
kyab sum kun du la ma sang gye la
go sum go pay go nay sol wa deb
rang zhen min gyi drup par jin gyi lob
chog dang tun mong ngo drub tsal du sol

Nine-line Request to Je Tsongkhapa

Buddha Vajradhara, the source of all-powerful attainments,
Avalokiteshvara, great treasure of objectless compassion,
Manjushri, master of flawless wisdom,
Vajrapani, destroyer of all demonic forces,
Losang Dragpa, crown jewel of the Snowy Lands' sages,
O Guru-Buddha, the embodiment of all three refuges
I humbly request you with my three doors:
Please grant inspiration to ripen myself and others
And bestow the general and supreme powerful attainments.

Recite any of the above verses continuously while doing the following visualizations:

Purification visualization

In the space in front of you is Je Tsongkhapa, the embodiment of Manjushri. On his right is Gyalsabje, the embodiment of Chenrezig, and on his left is Kedrupje, the embodiment of Vajrapani.[2] From these three, tubes of white light are emitted. They merge to form one and then flow into your heart. White nectar, like pure milk, flows through them into you and purifies all disease, spirit harms, destructive karmas, and obscurations. While reciting the request, first concentrate on purifying destructive karma created with the guru and the Three Jewels. Then concentrate on purifying destructive actions created with sentient beings.

After finishing the recitation, concentrate on your body being completely calm and clear, like crystal, completely free from all defilements.

30   LAMA TSONGKHAPA GURU YOGA

Visualizations to Generate Wisdom

1. Request, "Please inspire me to generate great wisdom that has no resistance to understanding the meaning of Buddha's extensive scriptures."

   From Je Tsongkhapa and his two spiritual children flows the orange nectar of great wisdom that fills your entire body. The essence of each atom of nectar is a small Manjushri. These Manjushris radiate light rays that touch the Buddhas and bodhisattvas in the ten directions. All of their wisdom, in the form of millions of Manjushris, absorbs into you through the pores of your body, like snow falling into the ocean. Feel that you have generated great wisdom.

2. Request, "Please inspire me to generate clear wisdom that can understand the subtle and difficult points of the Dharma without confusion."

   The visualization is the same as above, but the essence of each atom of nectar is Manjushri's mantra, *om ah ra pa tsa na dhi.* Millions of mantras are invoked from the Buddhas and bodhisattvas. They dissolve into you, and you generate clear wisdom.

3. Request, "Please inspire me to generate quick wisdom that quickly cuts off all ignorance, wrong conceptions, and doubt."

   Visualize as above, substituting Manjushri's seed syllable, DHI, and feel that you have generated quick wisdom.

LAMA TSONGKHAPA GURU YOGA   31

4. Request, "Please inspire me to generate profound wisdom that understands the meaning of the scriptures in a profound, limitless way."

Visualize as above, substituting Manjushri's implements, the sword and text, and feel that you have generated profound wisdom.

5. Request, "Please inspire me to generate the wisdom of explaining the Dharma that elucidates the definite, correct understanding of all the words and meanings of the scriptures."

Visualize as above, substituting texts, and feel you have generated the wisdom of explaining the Dharma.

6. Request, "Please inspire me to generate the wisdom of debate that courageously refutes the pernicious words that express wrong ideas."

Visualize as above, substituting eight-spoked wheels of swords, and feel that you have generated the wisdom of debate.

7. Request, "Please inspire me to generate the wisdom of composition, which uses perfect grammar and words and has the meaning of clear wisdom that gives joy."

Visualize as above, substituting texts and eight-spoked wheels of swords, and feel that you have generated the wisdom of composition.

If you wish, recite "The Foundation of All Good Qualities" or do a meditation on the stages of the path.

Requests

to sam gom pay shay rab pel du sol
che tso tsom pay lo dro gyay su sol
chog dang tun mong ngo drub tsel du sol
nyur du kye rang ta bur jin gyi lob

day chen lhen kye ye she char du sol
ngo dzin trul pal dri ma sel du sol
sem nyi tay tsom dra wa che du sol
nyur du kye rang ta bur jin gyi lob

Requests and Absorption

pal den tsa way la ma rin po che
dag gi chi wor pay may teng zug la
ka drin chen po go nay je zung te
ku sung tug kyi ngo drub tsal du sol

pal den tsa way la ma rin po che
dag gi nying kar pay may teng zug la
ka drin chen po go nay je zung te
chog dang tun mong ngo drup tsal du sol

pal den tsa way la ma rin po che
dag gi nying kar pay may teng zug la
ka drin chen po go nay je zung te
jang chub nying po bar du ten par zhug

Requests

May the wisdom of learning, thinking, and meditation increase,
And may the wisdom of teaching, debating, and writing increase.
May I attain the general and supreme powerful attainments.
Please inspire me to quickly become like you.

May the simultaneous-born great bliss shine immediately, and the
Afflicted shadow of grasping at inherent existence be cleared.
May I cut the net of doubt of the true nature of mind.
Please inspire me to quickly become like you.

Requests and Absorption

Glorious and precious root guru,
Sit upon the lotus and moon seat on my crown.
Guiding me with your great kindness,
Bestow upon me the attainments of your body, speech, and mind.

Glorious and precious root guru,
Sit upon the lotus and moon seat at my heart.
Guiding me with your great kindness,
Grant me the general and supreme powerful attainments.

Glorious and precious root guru,
Sit upon the lotus and moon seat at my heart.
Guiding me with your great kindness,
Please remain firmly until I attain full awakening.

Dedication

gay wa di yi nyur du dag
la ma sang gye drub gyur nay
dro wa chig kyang ma lu pa
kye kyi sa la go par shog

jang chub sem chog rin po che
ma kye pa nam kye gyur chig
kye pa nyam pa may pa yang
gong nay gong du pel war shog

dag gi ji nye sag pay gay wa di
ten dang dro wa kun la gang pen dang
kye par je tsun lo zang drag pa yi
ten pay nying po ring du sel jay shog

tse rab kun tu gyal wa tzong kha pay
teg chog shay nyen ngo su dze pay tu
gyal way ngag pay lam sang day nyi lay
ke chig tsam yang dog par mar gyur chig

Dedication

Due to this merit may we soon
Attain the awakened state of Guru-Buddha
That we may be able to liberate
All sentient beings from their sufferings.

May the precious bodhi mind
Not yet born arise and grow.
May that born have no decline
But increase forever more.

Whatever virtue I may have gathered here, may it bring benefit to the migrating beings and to the Buddha's teachings. May it make the essence of Buddha's doctrine, and especially the teachings of Venerable Losang Dragpa shine for a long time.

In all of my lives, through the Victorious One, Lama Tsongkhapa acting as the actual Mahayana guru, may I never turn away for even an instant from the excellent path praised by the Victorious Ones.

Vajrasattva Purification

The Power of Reliance: Taking Refuge and Generating Bodhicitta

Visualize a few inches above your head an open white lotus upon which is a moon disc. Vajrasattva is seated upon this. His body is made of white light and adorned with beautiful ornaments and clothes of celestial silk. His two hands are crossed at his heart; the right holds a vajra, the left holds a bell.[3] At his heart is a moon disc with the seed syllable HUM at its center and the letters of Vajrasattva's hundred-syllable mantra standing clockwise around its edge.

Holding this visualization clearly in your mind, contemplate and recite three times:

I take refuge in the Three Jewels. I will liberate all sentient beings and lead them to awakening. Thus, I perfectly generate the mind dedicated to attaining awakening for the benefit of all sentient beings.

The Power of Regret

Review harmful physical, verbal, and mental actions you have done, both those you can remember and those you created in previous lives but cannot recall. Generate deep regret for having done these. Have a strong wish to be free from their suffering results and to avoid causing harm to others and yourself in the future.

Seeing Vajrasattva as a combination of the wisdom and compassion of all the Buddhas and as your own wisdom and compassion in fully developed form, make this request:

38 VAJRASATTVA PURIFICATION

"O Bhagavan Vajrasattva, please clear away all negative karma and obscurations of myself and all living beings and purify all degenerated and broken commitments."

The Power of Remedial Action

From the HUM at Vajrasattva's heart, light radiates in all directions, requesting the Buddhas to bestow their inspiration. They accept the request and send white rays of light and nectar, the essence of which is the knowledge of their body, speech, and mind. The light and nectar absorb into the HUM and the letters of the mantra at Vajrasattva's heart. They then fill his entire body, enhancing the magnificence of his appearance and increasing the brilliance of the mantra.

While reciting the mantra, visualize that white rays of light and nectar stream continuously from the HUM and mantra at Vajrasattva's heart. They flow down through the crown of your head and fill every cell of your body and mind with infinite bliss. Recite the mantra at least 21 times, and more if possible:

om vajrasattva samaya manu palaya/ vajrasattva deno patita/ dido may bhawa/ suto kayo may bhawa/ supo kayo may bhawa/ anu rakto may bhawa/ sarwa siddhi mempar yatsa/ sarwa karma su tsa may/ tsitam shriyam kuru hum/ ha ha ha ha ho/ bhagawan/ sarwa tatagata/ vajra ma may mu tsa/ vajra bhawa maha samaya sattva/ ah hum pey

If you have not yet memorized the long mantra, or if you are pressed for time, you may recite the short mantra:

om vajrasattva hum

While reciting either of the mantras, continue to visualize the flow of light and nectar, and perform the following four visualizations alternately:

Purification of body. Your afflictions and negativities in general, and particularly those of the body, take the form of black ink. Sickness takes the form of pus and blood and disturbances caused by spirits appear in the form of scorpions, snakes, frogs, and crabs. Flushed out by the light and nectar, they leave your body through the lower openings, like filthy liquid flowing from a drainpipe. Feel completely empty of these problems and negativities; they no longer exist anywhere.

Purification of speech. Your afflictions and the latencies of negativities of speech take the form of liquid tar. The light and nectar fill your body as water fills a dirty glass: the negativities, like the dirt, rise to the top and flow out though the upper openings of your body—your eyes, ears, mouth, and nose. Feel completely empty of these negativities; they are gone forever.

Purification of mind. Your afflictions and the latencies of mental negativities appear as darkness at your heart. When struck by the forceful stream of light and nectar, the darkness instantly vanishes. It is like turning a light on in a room: the darkness does not go anywhere; it simply ceases to exist. Feel that you are completely empty of all of these negativities: they are non-existent.

Simultaneous purification. Do the three above visualizations simultaneously. This sweeps away the subtle obscurations that prevent you from seeing correctly all that exists. Feel completely free of these obscurations.

40   VAJRASATTVA PURIFICATION

The Power of Determination

Take refuge in Vajrasattva: "Through ignorance and delusion I have broken and degenerated my commitments. O spiritual master, be my protector and refuge. Lord, Holder of the Vajra, endowed with great compassion, in you, the foremost of beings, I take refuge."

Then make the determination: "I shall do my best not to do these destructive actions again in the future."

Vajrasattva is extremely pleased and says, "My spiritual child of the essence, all your negativities, obscurations, and degenerated vows have now been completely purified."

With delight, Vajrasattva melts into light and dissolves into you. Your body, speech, and mind become inseparable from Vajrasattva's holy body, speech, and mind. Concentrate on this.

Dedication

Due to this merit may we soon
Attain the awakened state of Vajrasattva
That we may be able to liberate
All sentient beings from their sufferings.

May the precious bodhi mind
Not yet born arise and grow.
May that born have no decline,
But increase forever more.

VAJRASATTVA PURIFICATION   41

Explanation of the mantra

Om: the qualities of the Buddha's holy body, speech, and mind; all that is auspicious and of great value.

Vajrasattva: the being who has the wisdom of inseparable bliss and emptiness.

Samaya: a pledge that cannot be transgressed.

Manupalaya: lead me along the path you took to awakening.

Vajrasattva deno patita: make me abide closer to Vajrasattva's vajra holy mind.

Dido may bhawa: please grant me the ability to have a firm and stable realization of the ultimate nature of phenomena.

Suto kayo may bhawa: please have the nature of being extremely pleased with me.

Supo kayo may bhawa: may I be in the nature of well-developed great bliss.

Anu rakto may bhawa: please have the nature of the love that leads me to your state.

Sarwa siddhi mempar yatsa: please grant me all powerful attainments.

Sarwa karma sutsa may: please grant me all virtuous actions.

Tsitam shriyam kuru: please grant me your glorious qualities.

Hum: the vajra holy mind.

42   VAJRASATTVA PURIFICATION

Ha ha ha ha ho: the five transcendental wisdoms.[4]

Bhagawan: one who has destroyed every obscuration, attained all realizations, and has passed beyond suffering.

Sarwa Tatagata: all those who have gone into the realization of emptiness, knowing things just as they are.

Vajra: inseparable, indestructible.

Ma may mu tsa: do not abandon me.

Vajra bhawa: the nature of inseparability.

Mahasamaya sattva: the great being who has the pledge, the vajra holy mind.

Ah: the vajra holy speech.

Hum: the transcendental wisdom of great bliss.

Pey: clarifies the transcendental wisdom of inseparable bliss and emptiness and destroys the dualistic mind that obstructs that.

Summary of the meaning of the mantra

O great being whose holy mind is in the indestructible nature of all the Buddhas, having destroyed every obscuration, attained all realizations and passed beyond all suffering, the one gone to the realization of things just as they are, do not forsake me. Please make me closer to your vajra holy mind, and grant me the ability to realize the ultimate nature of phenomena. Please help me to realize great bliss. Lead me to your state, and grant me all powerful attainments. Please bestow upon me all virtuous actions and glorious qualities.

Medicine Buddha Meditation

Above the crown of your head, upon a lotus and moon seat, is the Medicine Buddha. His body is made of blue light, and blue light radiates from him going in all directions. In the gesture of granting sublime realization, his right hand rests on his right knee and holds the stem of an arura plant. In the gesture of concentration, his left hand holds a lapis lazuli bowl filled with medicinal nectar. He is seated in the vajra posture, wears the three saffron robes of a monastic, and has the signs and marks of a Buddha.

Refuge and Bodhicitta

I take refuge until I have awakened in the Buddhas, the Dharma, and the Sangha. By the merit I create by engaging in generosity and the other far-reaching practices, may I attain Buddhahood in order to benefit all sentient beings. (3x)

May all sentient beings have happiness and its causes.
May all sentient beings be free of suffering and its causes.
May all sentient beings not be separated from sorrowless bliss.
May all sentient beings abide in equanimity, free of bias, attachment, and anger.

Seven-Limb Prayer

Reverently I prostrate with my body, speech, and mind to Guru Medicine Buddha,
And present clouds of every type of offering, actual and mentally transformed.
I confess all my destructive actions accumulated since beginningless time,
And rejoice in the virtues of all holy and ordinary beings.

Please remain until cyclic existence ends,
And turn the wheel of Dharma for sentient beings.
I dedicate all the virtues of myself and others to the
great awakening.

Mandala Offering

This ground, anointed with perfume, flowers strewn,
Mount Meru, four lands, sun and moon,
Imagined as a Buddha land and offered to you.
May all beings enjoy this pure land.

The objects of attachment, aversion, and ignorance—friends, enemies and strangers, my body, wealth, and enjoyments—I offer these without any sense of loss. Please accept them with pleasure, and inspire me and others to be free from the three poisonous attitudes.

Idam guru ratna mandalakam nirya tayami

Requests

I request you, Bhagawan Master of Healing, whose sky-colored holy body of lapis lazuli signifies omniscient wisdom and compassion as vast as limitless space, please inspire my mind.

I request you, compassionate Master of Healing, holding in your right hand the king of medicines symbolizing your vow to help all the sentient beings plagued by the 404 diseases, please inspire my mind.

I request you, compassionate Master of Healing, holding in your left hand a bowl of nectar symbolizing your vow to give the glorious undying nectar of the Dharma, which eliminates the degenerations of sickness, aging, and death, please inspire my mind.

46   MEDICINE BUDDHA MEDITATION

I prostrate, go for refuge, and make offerings to the fully realized destroyer of all defilements, completely perfected Buddha, who has realized the ultimate nature of all phenomena, Medicine Buddha, the King of Lapis Light. May your vow to benefit all sentient beings now ripen for myself and others. (3x or 7x)

Visualization and Mantra Recitation

In response to your request, infinite white rays of light stream down from the heart and body of the King of Medicine. Completely filling your body from head to toe, the light purifies all disease, afflictions due to interfering forces, and the negative karma and mental obscurations that cause these. All anxiety, fear, and negative emotions are also purified. These leave you in the form of dirty liquid, which then completely disappears. Your body becomes the nature of light, clean and clear like crystal.

Again light from the Medicine Buddha fills your body, bringing with it the realizations of the path and all the good qualities of the Buddhas and bodhisattvas. Your mind is transformed into love, compassion, and wisdom.

Visualize the Medicine Buddha on the crown of each sentient being's head. You may think specifically of those who are suffering and in need of healing now. Do a similar visualization as above, with the light first purifying their diseases and their causes and then bringing them the realizations of the path to awakening.

While doing these visualizations recite the mantra as much as possible:

tayata om bhekandze bhekandze maha bhekandze randza samungate soha

Absorption

After reciting the mantra, the Medicine Buddha melts into light and absorbs into your heart. Your mind becomes non-dual with the Buddha's dharmakaya mind. Similarly the Medicine Buddha on the crown of each sentient being's head melts into light and absorbs into the heart of that sentient being, bringing him or her infinite peace, compassion, and wisdom.

Dedication

Due to this merit may we soon
Attain the awakened state of Medicine Buddha
That we may be able to liberate
All sentient beings from their suffering.

May the precious bodhi mind
Not yet born arise and grow.
May that born have no decline,
But increase forever more.

Just as Guru Medicine Buddha, with compassion, guides all sentient beings, infinite as space, may I also become a compassionate guide of sentient beings existing in all directions of the universe.

White Tara Meditation

Refuge and Bodhicitta

I take refuge until I have awakened in the Buddhas, the Dharma and the Sangha. By the merit I create by engaging in generosity and the other far-reaching practices, may I attain Buddhahood in order to benefit all sentient beings. (3x)

May all sentient beings have happiness and its causes.
May all sentient beings be free of suffering and its causes.
May all sentient beings not be separated from sorrowless bliss.
May all sentient beings abide in equanimity, free of bias, attachment, and anger.

Visualization and Mantra Recitation

Above the crown of your head, the transcendental wisdom of all the Buddhas manifests as White Tara. Her body is in the nature of radiant white light. She has one face and two arms. Her right hand is on her right knee in the gesture of granting supreme realizations, and her left hand at her heart holds the stem of an utpala flower. Youthful and beautiful, she is seated in the vajra posture. She has all the signs and marks of a Buddha and has seven eyes (face, palms, soles, third eye). She looks at you and all sentient beings with complete acceptance and compassion.

At Tara's heart is a horizontal white moon disk. At its center is the white syllable TAM, the essence of her enlightened realizations. Light rays shine forth from the TAM, and hook back all the life force that has been scattered or lost. This dissolves into the TAM, in the form of light. Again light rays radiate from the TAM, and hook back the power and inspiration of all the Buddhas, bodhisattvas, and those who have attained the realization of long

MEDITATION ON WHITE TARA

life. This dissolves into the TAM. Also, the essence of the four elements of earth, water, fire, and air, as well as the space element, absorb into the TAM in the form of five-colored nectar-light (white, yellow, red, green, and blue).

From the TAM at her heart, light and nectar now flow into your body. They fill your entire body, dispelling all negative karma, disturbing attitudes, negative emotions, disease, interferences, and dangers of untimely death. All these leave your body in the form of dirty liquid, and your body becomes pure and clear. Your mind, too, becomes clear and blissful.

While doing this visualization, recite 21 times:

om tare tuttare ture mama ayur punye jnana pushtim kuru soha

50   MEDITATION ON WHITE TARA

Then recite as much as possible:

om tare tuttare ture soha

Think and feel, "I am liberated from all negative karma, afflictions, negative emotions, disease, interferences and dangers of untimely death. I will use my life in a meaningful way to transform my mind; develop love, compassion, and the six far-reaching practices; and act in ways that benefit others, myself, and our environment."

Dedication

Due to this merit may we soon
Attain the awakened state of White Tara
That we will be able to liberate
All sentient beings from their suffering.

May anyone who merely sees, hears, remembers, touches or talks to me be freed in that very instant from all sufferings and abide in happiness forever.

May the glorious spiritual mentors live long, and may all beings throughout limitless space be happy. By purifying our defilements and accumulating merit, may I and all others be inspired to attain Buddhahood quickly.

In order to train just like the hero Manjushri, who knows reality as it is, and just like Samantabhadra as well, I completely dedicate all this goodness, just as they did.

With that dedication which is praised as greatest by all the Buddhas gone to freedom in the three times, I, too, dedicate all my roots of goodness for the attainments of the bodhisattva practice.

Meditation on Amitabha Buddha

Taking Refuge, Generating the Altruistic Intention, and the Four Immeasurables

I take refuge until I have awakened in the Buddhas, the Dharma, and the Sangha. By the merit I create by engaging in generosity and the other far-reaching practices, may I attain Buddhahood in order to benefit all sentient beings. (3x)

May all sentient beings have happiness and its causes.
May all sentient beings be free of suffering and it causes.
May all sentient beings not be separated from sorrowless bliss.
May all sentient beings abide in equanimity, free of bias, attachment, and anger.

Visualization of Guru Amitabha Buddha

Visualize the following with single pointed clarity.

Above my crown on a lotus, moon, and sun sits Guru Amitabha Buddha in the vajra pose. His holy body is radiant and ruby red. He has one face and two hands resting in the gesture of meditation.

Holding an alms bowl filled with the elixir of immortality, he wears the saffron robes of ethical purity. His crown is marked by a shining white OM, his throat by a radiant red AH, and his heart by a blue HUM.

From the HUM in his heart, boundless light shines forth filling all of space. This light especially penetrates Amitabha's Pure Land, invoking Amitabha Buddha, the eight great lion-like bodhisattvas, as well as the vast assembly of male and female bodhisattvas who reside in the Land of Great Bliss. These all enter Guru Amitabha's crown chakra, descend his central channel, and absorb into his heart. They are unified and of one nature.

Hold this thought with single-pointed concentration.

MEDITATION ON AMITABHA BUDDHA   53

Seven-Limb Prayer

I prostrate with my body, speech, and mind in heartfelt faith
and admiration,
And make actual and mentally imagined exquisite offerings
that fill the sky.
I reveal and confess every destructive action I have done since
beginningless time,
And rejoice in the countless virtues done by ordinary beings and
the inconceivable virtues accumulated by aryas.
Please, Guru Amitabha, remain in your present vajra form until
cyclic existence ends,
And turn the wheel of Dharma to benefit sentient beings.
I dedicate all past, present, and future virtues of myself and others
to full awakening.

Mandala Offering

This ground, anointed with perfume, flowers strewn,
Mount Meru, four lands, sun and moon,
Imagined as a Buddha land and offered to you.
May all beings enjoy this pure land.

The objects of attachment, aversion, and ignorance—friends,
enemies and strangers, my body, wealth, and enjoyments—I offer
these without any sense of loss. Please accept them with pleasure
and inspire me and others to be free from the three poisonous
attitudes.

idam guru ratna mandalakam nirya tayami

Prostrations (optional)

To the guru, teacher, endowed transcendent destroyer, one thus
gone, foe destroyer, completely and fully awakened one,
magnificent king, Guru Amitabha of boundless light, I prostrate,
make offerings, and go for refuge. Please bestow upon me great
inspiration.

54 MEDITATION ON AMITABHA BUDDHA

Mantra Recitation

With heart-felt devotion I concentrate single-pointedly on Guru Amitabha. From his holy body, five-colored nectar light streams down into my crown, descending through my central channel. From there it flows through all the other channels of my body, completely filling it with blissful nectar and light. All hindrances, illness, and untimely death are completely purified. All negative emotions and disturbing attitudes, especially grasping at true existence, totally disappear. My body becomes crystal clear like a rainbow, and my mind becomes peaceful and free from craving.

Om amideva hrih

Recite the mantra as many times as you like, while continuing to do the visualization. At the end of the recitation, rest the mind single-pointedly on Amitabha and feel completely free from obscurations.

Aspirations

All past, present, and future gurus, Buddhas, and bodhisattvas dwelling in the ten directions of space, especially Amitabha Buddha and the eight great lion-like bodhisattvas, please pay attention to me. Wishing to liberate all mother sentient beings from the vast ocean of samsaric suffering and to lead them to the supreme joy of full awakening, I realize that I must become a Buddha. In order to do that, I determine to take rebirth in the Land of Great Bliss and to hear teachings directly from Amitabha Buddha himself. Therefore, by the force of all my past, present, and future merit collected together, the immutable promise of all the Tathagatas, and the power of wisdom and ultimate truth may I, at the very moment of death, take immediate and spontaneous rebirth upon a fully opened lotus in the presence of Amitabha Buddha's radiant form. Without difficulty, may I hear teachings directly from Amitabha Buddha.

MEDITATION ON AMITABHA BUDDHA   55

May I develop the six far-reaching practices to their ultimate completion, and may I accomplish the ten bodhisattva stages. May I attain the wisdom, love, and power of myriads of Buddhas in countless Buddha-fields more numerous than all the atoms of the universe.

Since time without beginning, I have been confused and have circled in samsaric suffering. Bound by craving and grasping, I have experienced continuous misery. Unless I release this deluded and grasping mind, the Buddhas and bodhisattvas cannot be of ultimate benefit to me. Nothing in samsara is certain except that all mundane pleasures die away. This grasping and ignorant mind is the noose that binds me to the relentless turning of the wheel of conditioned existence. I yearn to go to Amitabha's Pure Land, where even the word "suffering" does not exist, and from where I can again never fall into samsara's misery.

The Prayer for the Time of Death (optional)

At the moment the messenger of death arrives, please come instantaneously from your pristine realm, advise me to give up grasping at mundane existence, and invite me to come to your pristine realm.

When the earth absorbs into water, the mirage-like appearance is perceived, and my mouth becomes dry and foul-tasting, please come tell me not to be afraid and inspire me with true courage.

When water absorbs into fire, the smoke-like appearance is perceived, and my tongue gets thick and my speech is lost, please show me your shining face and give me solace and peaceful joy.

56   MEDITATION ON AMITABHA BUDDHA

When fire absorbs into air, the firefly-like appearance is perceived, and my body heat and the light of my eyes rapidly fade away, please come and fill my mind with the sound of Dharma wisdom.

When air absorbs into consciousness, the burning like a butter lamp appearance is perceived, and my body becomes like the earth and my breathing altogether ceases, please draw me to your pure land with the radiant light of your shining face.

Then may the radiant red hook emanating from your pristine heart enter my crown, descend my central channel, and hook my very subtle clear light mind and bring it to your pure land.

Yet, if I must go into the intermediate state by the force of my destructive karma, may all the Buddhas and bodhisattvas rescue me with the power of Dharma and inspire me with the pure view that sees all beings as utterly pure, hears all sounds as Dharma teaching, and sees all places as a pure land.

Absorption

The lotus, moon, and sun, as well as Guru Amitabha melt into light and dissolve into my heart center. Guru Amitabha's mind and my mind become non-dual.

Rest the mind in the experience of being non-dual with Guru Amitabha's realizations.

MEDITATION ON AMITABHA BUDDHA   57

Dedication

Due to this merit may we soon
Attain the awakened state of Amitabha
That we may be able to liberate
All sentient beings from their sufferings.

May the precious bodhi mind
Not yet born arise and grow.
May that born have no decline
But increase forever more.

Due to the merit accumulated by myself and others in the past, present, and future, may anyone who merely sees, hears, remembers, touches or talks to me be freed in that very instant from all sufferings and abide in happiness forever.

In all rebirths, may I and all sentient beings be born in a good family, have clear wisdom and great compassion, be free of pride and devoted to our spiritual mentors, and abide within the vows and commitments to our spiritual mentors.

By the force of these praises and requests made to you, may all disease, poverty, fighting, and quarrels be calmed. May the Dharma and all auspiciousness increase throughout the worlds and directions where I and all others dwell.

Colophon
This sadhana composed in 1981 at Tushita Retreat Center by Lama Thubten Yeshe in accordance with the scriptures and oral transmission. Abbreviated by Ven. Thubten Chodron.

Prayer to be Reborn in the Land of Bliss
By Je Tsongkhapa

With deeds exalted, you grant splendor unending. Once remembered, you hurl far all fear of the lord of death. With constant love, you look on others as sons and daughters. Amitayus, teacher of gods and humans, I bow before you.

Swayed by compassion I will write as best I can a prayer for birth in Sukhavati, land of bliss, praised again and again by the mighty Buddha as the highest of realms.

All knowledge of what to practice and what to abandon is covered by layers of ignorance. All future lives in higher realms are slain by the weapons of anger. Lying trussed by the ropes of desire in the prison of samsara, I am carried helplessly to the oceans of cyclic existence by rivers of karma. Tossed by endless waves of aging, sickness, and other suffering, thrown to the jaws of that savage monster the lord of death, I languish under the weight of unwanted suffering.

PRAYER TO BE REBORN IN THE LAND OF BLISS 59

Without a protector and with anguished cries I ask with devotion, as witnesses to the yearnings of my mind, Amitabha, guide and sole friend to the deprived; powerful Avalokiteshvara Bodhisattva, Vajrapani and entourage to not forget the vows of the supreme bodhicitta made over countless eons for our sakes. Like the mighty garuda hawk swooping through the skies, please come before me through your miraculous power and great compassion.

By the power of the immense twin accumulation of spiritual merit created by myself and others in the past, present, and future, I pray that when death draws near I see before me my guide Amitabha, his two main disciples, his entourage, and other holy beings. At that time may I have strong faith in this great conqueror and his entourage and be free from the pain of dying.

By recalling and holding in my mind these objects of faith, I pray that as soon as my consciousness has left this body, the eight bodhisattvas arrive by miraculous power to show the way to Sukhavati, there to be born within a jeweled lotus, with sharp faculties and in the Mahayana family.

Once born in Sukhavati, may I gain immediately the powerful dharani memory, meditative concentration, objectless bodhicitta, inexhaustible confidence, and countless other qualities. By pleasing the highest of teachers, Amitabha and all Buddhas and bodhisattvas of the ten directions, may I take with propriety the Mahayana teachings.

When I have absorbed and understood the true meanings of these teachings, may I be able to travel in an instant and without hindrance to limitless Buddha realms by miraculous power, there to perfect every powerful practice of the bodhisattva.

Though born in pure Sukhavati, I pray to be able to journey to impure realms with unhindered miraculous power motivated by fierce compassion, there to teach every living being the Dharma according to their disposition and so bring them to that immaculate path hailed by the Buddha. By quickly perfecting these exalted practices, for the benefit of countless living beings, may I easily attain the awakened state of a Buddha.

When the amalgamations of this life are spent, may I plainly behold in my path of vision Amitabha encircled by a vast entourage, and may my mind be filled with faith and compassion.

Once the bardo visions have appeared, may I be shown the path by the eight bodhisattvas and, born in Sukhavati, by manifestation may I become a spiritual guide for impure realms.

Should I not attain such exalted states, in every life may I be born solely in a form capable of engaging in authentic study, contemplation, and meditation upon the transmitted and realized Buddhadharma.

May that form be always endowed with the seven desirable features of higher realms. In every such existence may I gain the memory that recalls perfectly all my past lives. In every life may I see all samsaric existence as being without essence, be motivated by a mind captivated by the virtues of nirvana, and be ordained into the monastic discipline so excellently taught by the Buddha. Once ordained, may I live as the monk Akshobhya who, unsullied by the slightest fault, perfected ethical conduct and gained great awakening.

PRAYER TO BE REBORN IN THE LAND OF BLISS   61

Furthermore, having fully comprehended the ways of afflictive states of mind and the paths of purification and freedom, in every life may I develop the powerful and accomplished dharani memory to maintain total recall over every word and meaning of every branch and division of the teachings. In the same way that I retain these dharmas, may I gain a pure and unhindered confidence to teach them likewise to others.

Furthermore, in every life may I master and never be apart from the ways of meditative concentrations such as the heroic shurangama samadhi. May I acquire supernormal sight such as that unhindered by matter, as well as the superknowledges such as knowing the ways of miraculous powers.

Furthermore, in every life may I develop that great wisdom that, self-reliantly and unaided, is able to differentiate what to practice and what to abandon.

May I develop the clear wisdom that unerringly separates even the subtlest degree of afflictive mental states from paths of purification and freedom.

May I develop the quick wisdom that holds the power to counter all doubts, fallacious views, and incomprehension as soon as they appear.

May I develop the profound wisdom that penetrates without obstacle the meanings of scripture unfathomable to others.

In short, with wisdom stripped of all afflictive intelligence may I rise to the wisdom skillful in unlocking the meanings of scripture in order to attain the perfection of every bodhisattva practice just as the noble Manjushri has done.

62 PRAYER TO BE REBORN IN THE LAND OF BLISS

Having gained without difficulty great, clear, quick, and profound wisdom, may I, in order to gather the fortunate, to crush false orators, and to please the wise, perfect the arts of teaching, debating, and composition that focus upon the complete teachings of the Buddha.

Furthermore, in every life, having put an end to all self-preoccupied ways of thinking and to all laziness and weakness regarding the powerful practices of the bodhisattva, may I possess bodhicitta wise in the accomplishment of supreme courage and the willingness to dedicate myself to others. As the noble Avalokiteshvara has done, may I perfect every bodhisattva practice.

Furthermore, in every life, whenever I apply myself to the welfare of self and others, may I possess a skillful ability to demolish all negative forces, defeat those holding extreme views, and thwart all opponents. As the noble Vajrapani has done, may I perfect all the bodhisattva practices.

To perfect the bodhisattva practice that dispels all laziness, may I in every life first generate bodhicitta, and by powerful endeavor undistracted for even an instant, may I reach great awakening as the unparalleled Shakyamuni has done.

To eradicate obstacles to practices of awakening, such as sickness of body or mind, may I, in every life, pacify, as does the King of Physicians, the Medicine Buddha, all pain of body, speech, and mind merely by mentioning his name.

Furthermore, in all lifetimes may I have the power to live out my lifespan as I wish and, merely by mentioning his name, may I destroy all untimely death as the conqueror Amitayus does.

PRAYER TO BE REBORN IN THE LAND OF BLISS   63

Whenever life-threatening obstacles arise, may I behold with clarity in whatever manifestation is appropriate, Amitayus, who curbs the threat by way of the four awakening activities. With such a vision, may every hindrance to life be at once removed.

Recognizing such an appropriate manifestation to be none other than Amitayus, may I develop unshakable, uncontrived faith by whose power I will forever be in the presence of Amitayus as my spiritual teacher.

Furthermore, in life after life, by pleasing him in return, may I be forever fostered by accomplished Mahayana spiritual masters, the source of every virtue of this world and beyond. In their care, may I acquire a firm unshakable faith in them, pleasing them by every means possible, doing nothing, even for an instant, to disappoint them.

May my spiritual masters impart to me every instruction and teaching in its entirety. Having understood them faultlessly, may I practice them and be able to bring them to perfection. May I never, even for a moment, fall under the sway of malevolent teachers and misleading friends.

In every life, having developed belief in cause and effect, renunciation, bodhicitta, and the correct view, may I embark upon them continually with effortless experience. In all lives may every virtuous action accumulated by body, speech, and mind be causes solely for the fulfillment of others' welfare and for the purest and highest awakening.

Reprinted from *The Splendor of an Autumn Moon: The Devotional Verse of Tsongkhapa,* translated by Gavin Kilty, published by Wisdom Publications. Prayer edited for *Pearl of Wisdom Book II* by Ven. Thubten Chodron.

The King of Prayers
The Extraordinary Aspiration of the Practice of Samantabhadra

I bow down to the youthful Arya Manjushri.

You lions among humans,
Gone to freedom in the present, past and future
In the worlds of ten directions,
To all of you, with body, speech, and sincere mind I bow down.

With the energy of aspiration for the bodhisattva way,
With a sense of deep respect,
And with as many bodies as atoms of the world,
To all you Buddhas visualized before me, I bow down.

On every atom are Buddhas numberless as atoms,
Each amidst a host of bodhisattvas,
And I am confident the sphere of all phenomena
Is entirely filled with Buddhas in this way.

With infinite oceans of praise for you,
And oceans of sound from the aspects of my voice,
I sing the breathtaking excellence of Buddhas,
And celebrate all of you Gone to Bliss.

Beautiful flowers and regal garlands,
Sweet music, scented oils and parasols,
Sparkling lights and sublime incense,
I offer to you Victorious Ones.

Fine dress and fragrant perfumes,
Sandalwood powder heaped high as Mount Meru,
All wondrous offerings in spectacular array,
I offer to you Victorious Ones.

THE KING OF PRAYERS 65

With transcendent offerings peerless and vast,
With profound admiration for all the Buddhas,
With strength of conviction in the bodhisattva way,
I offer and bow down to all Victorious Ones.

Every harmful action I have done
With my body, speech and mind
Overwhelmed by attachment, anger and confusion,
All these I openly lay bare before you.

I lift up my heart and rejoice in all merit
Of the Buddhas and bodhisattvas in ten directions,
Of solitary realizers, hearers still training and those beyond,
And of all ordinary beings.

You who are the bright lights of worlds in ten directions,
Who have attained a Buddha's omniscience through the stages
of awakening,
All you who are my guides,
Please turn the supreme wheel of Dharma.

With palms together I earnestly request:
You who may actualize parinirvana,
Please stay with us for eons numberless as atoms of the world,
For the happiness and well-being of all wanderers in samsara.

Whatever slight merit I may have created,
By paying homage, offering, and acknowledging my faults,
Rejoicing, and requesting that the Buddhas stay and teach,
I now dedicate all this for full awakening.

May you Buddhas now living in the worlds of ten directions,
And all you gone to freedom in the past, accept my offerings.
May those not yet arisen quickly perfect their minds,
Awakening as fully enlightened ones.

66   THE KING OF PRAYERS

May all worlds in ten directions,
Be entirely pure and vast.
May they be filled with bodhisattvas
Surrounding Buddhas gathered beneath a bodhi tree.

May as many beings as exist in ten directions
Be always well and happy.
May all samsaric beings live in accord with the Dharma,
And may their every Dharma wish be fulfilled.

Remembering my past lives in all varieties of existence,
May I practice the bodhisattva way,
And thus, in each cycle of death, migration, and birth,
May I always abandon the householder's life.

Then, following in the footsteps of all the Buddhas,
And perfecting the practice of a bodhisattva,
May I always act without error or compromise,
With ethical conduct faultless and pure.

May I teach the Dharma in the language of gods,
In every language of spirits and nagas,
Of humans and of demons,
And in the voice of every form of being.

May I be gentle-minded, cultivating the six paramitas,
And never forget bodhicitta.
May I completely cleanse without omission
Every negativity and all that obscures this awakening mind.

May I traverse all my lives in the world,
Free of karma, afflictions, and interfering forces,
Just as the lotus blossom is undisturbed by the water's wave,
Just as the sun and moon move unhindered through the sky.

THE KING OF PRAYERS   67

May I ease the suffering in the lower realms
And in the many directions and dimensions of the universe.
May I guide all wanderers in samsara to the pure bliss of awakening
And be of worldly benefit to them as well.

May I practice constantly for eons to come,
Perfecting the activities of awakening,
Acting in harmony with the various dispositions of beings,
Showing the ways of a bodhisattva.

May I always have the friendship
Of those whose path is like mine,
And with body, words, and also mind,
May we practice together the same aspirations and activities.

May I always meet a spiritual mentor
And never displease that excellent friend,
Who deeply wishes to help me
And expertly teaches the bodhisattva way.

May I always directly see the Buddhas,
Masters encircled by bodhisattvas,
And without pause or discouragement for eons to come,
May I make extensive offerings to them.

May I hold within me the Buddha's genuine Dharma,
Illuminate everywhere the teachings that awaken,
Embody the realizations of a bodhisattva,
And practice ardently in all future eons.

While circling through all states of existence,
May I become an endless treasure of good qualities—
Skillful means, wisdom, samadhi, and liberating stabilizations—
Gathering limitless pristine wisdom and merit.

68   THE KING OF PRAYERS

On one atom I shall see
Buddha fields numberless as atoms,
Inconceivable Buddhas among bodhisattvas in every field,
Practicing the activities of awakening.

Perceiving this in all directions,
I dive into an ocean of Buddha fields,
Each an ocean of three times Buddhas in the space of a wisp of hair.
So I, too, will practice for an ocean of eons.

Thus I am continually immersed in the speech of the Buddhas,
Expression that reveals an ocean of qualities in one word,
The completely pure eloquence of all the Buddhas,
Communication suited to the varied tendencies of beings.

With strength of understanding I plunge
Into the infinite awakened speech of the Dharma
Of all Buddhas in three times gone to freedom,
Who continually turn the wheel of Dharma methods.

I shall experience in one moment
Such vast activity of all future eons,
And I will enter into all eons of the three times,
In but a fraction of a second.

In one instant I shall see all those awakened beings,
Past, present, and future lions among humans,
And with the power of the illusion-like stabilization,
I will constantly engage in their inconceivable activity.

I shall manifest upon one single atom
The array of pure lands present, past, and future.
Likewise, I shall enter the array of pure Buddha fields
In every direction without exception.

THE KING OF PRAYERS 69

I shall enter the very presence of all my guides,
Those lights of this world who are yet to appear,
Those sequentially turning the wheels of complete awakening,
Those who reveal nirvana—final, perfect peace.

May I achieve the power of swift, magical emanation,
The power to lead to the great vehicle through every approach,
The power of always-beneficial activity,
The power of love pervading all realms,
The power of all-surpassing merit,
The power of supreme knowledge unobstructed by discrimination,
And through the powers of wisdom, skillful means, and samadhi,
May I achieve the perfect power of awakening.

Purifying the power of all contaminated actions,
Crushing the power of disturbing emotions at their root,
Defusing the power of interfering forces,
I shall perfect the power of the bodhisattva practice.

May I purify an ocean of worlds,
May I free an ocean of beings,
May I clearly see an ocean of Dharma,
May I realize an ocean of pristine wisdom.

May I purify an ocean of activities,
May I fulfill an ocean of aspirations,
May I make offerings to an ocean of Buddhas,
May I practice without discouragement for an ocean of eons.

To awaken fully through this bodhisattva way,
I shall fulfill without exception
All the diverse aspirations of the awakening practice
Of all Buddhas gone to freedom in the three times everywhere.

In order to practice exactly as the wise one
Called Samantabhadra, "All-Embracing Good,"
The elder brother of the sons and daughters of the Buddhas,
I completely dedicate all this goodness.

70   THE KING OF PRAYERS

Likewise may I dedicate,
Just as the skillful Samantabhadra,
For pure body, speech, and mind,
Pure actions and pure Buddha fields.

I shall give rise to the aspirations of Manjushri
For this bodhisattva practice of all-embracing good,
To perfect these practices
Without discouragement or pause in all future eons.

May my pure activities be endless,
My good qualities boundless,
And through abiding in immeasurable activity,
May I actualize infinite emanations.

Limitless is the end of space.
Likewise, limitless are living beings.
Thus, limitless are karma and afflictions.
May my aspiration's reach be limitless as well.

One may offer to the Buddhas
All wealth and adornments of infinite worlds in ten directions,
And one may offer during eons numberless as atoms of the world
Even the greatest happiness of gods and humans;

But whoever hears this extraordinary aspiration,
And longing for highest awakening
Gives rise to faith just once,
Creates far more precious merit.

Those who make this heartfelt aspiration for the bodhisattva way
Will be free of all lower rebirths,
Free of harmful companions,
And will quickly see Amitabha, Infinite Light.

THE KING OF PRAYERS   71

And even in this very human life,
They will be nourished by happiness and have all conducive
circumstances.
Without waiting long,
They will become like Samantabhadra himself.

Those who give voice to this extraordinary aspiration
Will quickly and completely purify
The five boundless harmful actions
Created under the power of ignorance.

Blessed with supreme knowledge,
Excellent body, family, attributes, and appearance,
They will be invincible to vast interfering forces and misleading
teachers,
And all the three worlds will make offerings.

Going quickly to the noble bodhi tree,
And sitting there to benefit sentient beings,
Subduing all interfering forces,
They will fully awaken and turn the great wheel of Dharma.

Have no doubt that complete awakening
Is the fully ripened result—comprehended only by a Buddha—
Of holding in mind by teaching, reading, or reciting
This aspiration of the bodhisattva practice.

In order to train just like
The hero Manjushri who knows reality as it is,
And just like Samantabhadra as well,
I completely dedicate all this goodness, just as they did.

With that dedication which is praised as greatest
By all the Buddhas gone to freedom in the three times,
I, too, dedicate all my roots of goodness
For the attainments of the bodhisattva practice.

72   THE KING OF PRAYERS

When the moment of my death arrives,
By eliminating all obscurations
And directly perceiving Amitabha,
May I go immediately to Sukhavati, Pure Land of Great Joy.

Having gone to Sukhavati,
May I actualize the meaning of these aspirations,
Fulfilling them all without exception,
For the benefit of beings for as long as this world endures.

Born from an extremely beautiful, superlative lotus
In this joyful land, the Buddha's magnificent mandala,
May I receive a prediction of my awakening
Directly from the Buddha Amitabha.

Having received a prediction there,
May I create vast benefit
For beings throughout the ten directions,
With a billion emanations by the power of wisdom.

Through even the small virtue I have accumulated
By offering this prayer of the bodhisattva practice,
May all the positive aspirations of beings
Be fulfilled in an instant.

Through creating limitless merit
By dedicating this prayer of Samantabhadra's deeds,
May all beings drowning in this torrent of suffering
Enter the presence of Amitabha.

Through this king of aspirations, which is the greatest of the sublime,
Helping infinite wanderers in samsara,
Through the accomplishment of this scripture dazzling with
Samantabhadra's practice,
May suffering realms be utterly emptied of all beings.

Aspiring and Engaging Bodhicitta

There are two levels in the development of bodhicitta—the mind dedicated to attaining awakening for the benefit of all sentient beings. These are the aspiring and engaging bodhicitta. A person with the aspiring bodhicitta wants to attain awakening for the benefit of all sentient beings, but he or she is not yet prepared to engage in all the practices necessary to do so.

A person who has generated the engaging bodhicitta joyfully engages in the bodhisattva's six far-reaching practices by taking the bodhisattva precepts. The difference between aspiring and engaging bodhicitta is similar to the difference between wanting to go to Dharamsala and actually getting on the transport and traveling there.

The bodhisattva precepts are taken on the basis of having taken refuge in the Three Jewels and some or all of the five lay precepts.

Generating Aspiring Bodhicitta

With the wish to free all sentient beings,
I take refuge at all times
In the Buddhas, Dharma, and Sangha
Until attainment of full awakening.

Today in the presence of the awakened ones,
Inspired by compassion, wisdom, and joyous effort,
I generate the mind aspiring for full Buddhahood
For the well-being of all sentient beings.

For as long as space endures,
And as long as sentient beings remain,
Until then may I too abide
To dispel the misery of the world.

Taking the Bodhisattva Vow

Those who have taken the bodhisattva vow should renew it every morning and evening by reciting and contemplating the following verses.

Spiritual mentors, Buddhas, and bodhisattvas, please listen to what I now say from the depths of my heart. Just as the sugatas of the past have developed bodhicitta and just as they practiced step-by-step in the bodhisattvas' trainings, so I, too, for the sake of benefiting migrating beings, will cultivate bodhicitta and practice step-by-step the trainings of the bodhisattvas. (3x)

At this moment my life has become fruitful.
I have attained a human existence,
And today I have been born in the Buddha's lineage
And have become the Buddhas' spiritual child.

Henceforth, whatever happens
I will undertake actions that accord with this lineage
And will act so as not to sully
This faultless venerable lineage.

ASPIRING AND ENGAGING BODHICITTA   75

The Eight Precepts of Aspiring Bodhicitta

After generating aspiring bodhicitta before your spiritual mentor and the Three Jewels, you should observe eight precepts in order to protect your bodhicitta from degenerating in this and future lives.

How to protect your bodhicitta from degenerating in this life:

1. Remember the advantages of bodhicitta repeatedly.

2. To strengthen your bodhicitta, generate the aspiration to attain awakening for the benefit of all sentient beings three times in the morning and three times in the evening. Recitation and contemplation of the verse for taking refuge and generating the bodhicitta is a good way to fulfill this.

3. Do not give up working for sentient beings even when they are harmful.

4. To enhance your bodhicitta, accumulate both merit and wisdom continuously.

How to prevent being separated from bodhicitta in future lives:

The four remaining precepts are explained in two complementary sets of four.

Abandon the four harmful actions:
1. Deceiving your guru, abbot, or other holy beings with lies.

2. Causing others to regret virtuous actions they have done.

3. Abusing or criticizing bodhisattvas or the Mahayana.

4. Not acting with a pure selfless wish but with pretension and deceit.

Practice the four constructive actions:

1. Abandon deliberately deceiving and lying to gurus, abbots and so forth.

2. Be straightforward, without pretension or deceit.

3. Generate recognition of bodhisattvas as your teachers and praise them.

4. Assume the responsibility yourself to lead all sentient beings to awakening.

The Bodhisattva Ethical Code[5]

The eighteen root bodhisattva precepts

When a precept has more than one aspect, doing just one aspect constitutes a transgression of the precept.

1. a) Praising yourself, or b) belittling others because of attachment to receiving material offerings, praise, and respect.

2. Not giving material aid, or b) not teaching the Dharma to those who are suffering and without a protector, because of miserliness.

3. Not listening although another declares his/her offence or b) with anger blaming him/her and retaliating.

4. Abandoning the Mahayana by saying that Mahayana texts are not the words of Buddha, or b) teaching what appears to be the Dharma but is not.

5. Taking things belonging to a) Buddha, b) Dharma, or c) Sangha.

ASPIRING AND ENGAGING BODHICITTA   77

6. Abandoning the holy Dharma by saying that texts that teach the three vehicles are not the Buddha's word.

7. With anger a) depriving ordained ones of their robes, beating and imprisoning them, or b) causing them to lose their ordination even if they have impure ethical conduct, for example, by saying that being ordained is useless.

8. Committing any of the five extremely destructive actions: a) killing your mother, b) killing your father, c) killing an arhat, d) intentionally drawing blood from a Buddha, or e) causing schism in the sangha community by supporting and spreading sectarian views.

9. Holding wrong views (contrary to the teachings of Buddha, such as denying the existence of the Three Jewels or the law of cause and effect, etc.)

10. Destroying a a) town, b) village, c) city, or d) large area by means such as fire, bombs, pollution, or black magic.

11. Teaching emptiness to those whose minds are unprepared.

12. Causing those who have entered the Mahayana to turn away from working for the full awakening of Buddhahood and encouraging them to work merely for their own liberation from suffering.

13. Causing others to abandon completely their precepts of self-liberation and embrace the Mahayana.

14. Holding and causing others to hold the view that the Fundamental Vehicle does not abandon attachment and other delusions.

78   ASPIRING AND ENGAGING BODHICITTA

15. Falsely saying that you have realized profound emptiness and that if others meditate as you have, they will realize emptiness and become as great and as highly realized as you.

16. Taking gifts from others who were encouraged to give you things originally intended as offerings to the Three Jewels. Not giving things to the Three Jewels that others have given you to give to them, or accepting property stolen from the Three Jewels.

17. a) Causing those engaged in serenity meditation to give it up by giving their belongings to those who are merely reciting texts or b) making bad disciplinary rules that cause a spiritual community not to be harmonious.

18. Abandoning the two bodhicittas (aspiring and engaging).

Four binding factors must be present to completely transgress sixteen of the root precepts. The transgression of two precepts, numbers 9 and 18, requires only the act itself. These four are:

1. Not regarding your action as destructive, or not caring that it is even though you recognize that the action is transgressing a precept.

2. Not abandoning the thought to do the action again.

3. Being happy and rejoicing in the action.

4. Not having a sense of integrity or consideration for others regarding what you have done.

To keep yourself from experiencing the results of transgressing the precepts, purify by means of the four opponent powers. Prostrations to the thirty-five Buddhas and the Vajrasattva

ASPIRING AND ENGAGING BODHICITTA   79

meditation are excellent methods to purify transgressions. If your bodhisattva ordination has been damaged by completely breaking a root precept, purify and then retake the precepts before a spiritual mentor or before the objects of refuge—the Buddhas and bodhisattvas—that you have visualized.

The forty-six auxiliary bodhisattva precepts

To eliminate obstacles to the far-reaching practice of generosity and obstacles to the ethical conduct of gathering virtuous actions, abandon:

1. Not making offerings to the Three Jewels every day with your body, speech, and mind.

2. Acting out selfish thoughts of desire to gain material possessions or reputation.

3. Not respecting your elders (those who have taken the bodhisattva precepts before you have or who have more experience than you do).

4. Not answering sincerely asked questions that you are capable of answering.

5. Not accepting invitations from others out of anger, pride, or other negative thoughts.

6. Not accepting gifts of money, gold, or other precious substances that others offer to you.

7. Not giving the Dharma to those who desire it.

80   ASPIRING AND ENGAGING BODHICITTA

To eliminate obstacles to the far-reaching practice of ethical conduct, abandon:

8. Forsaking those who have broken their ethical conduct: not giving them advice or not relieving their guilt.

9. Not acting in accord with your pratimoksa precepts.

10. Doing only limited actions to benefit sentient beings, such as strictly keeping the vinaya rules in situations when not doing so would be of greater benefit to others.

11. Not doing nonvirtuous actions of body and speech with loving compassion when circumstances deem it necessary in order to benefit others.

12. Willingly accepting things that either you or others have obtained by any of the wrong livelihoods of hypocrisy, hinting, flattery, coercion, or bribery.

13. Being distracted by and having a strong attachment to amusement, or without any beneficial purpose leading others to join in distracting activities.

14. Believing and saying that followers of the Mahayana should remain in cyclic existence and not try to attain liberation from afflictions.

15. Not abandoning destructive actions that cause you to have a bad reputation.

16. Not correcting your own afflictive actions or not helping others to correct theirs.

ASPIRING AND ENGAGING BODHICITTA   81

To eliminate obstacles to the far-reaching practice of fortitude, abandon:

17. Returning insults, anger, beating, or criticism with insults and the like.

18. Neglecting those who are angry with you by not trying to pacify their anger.

19. Refusing to accept the apologies of others.

20. Acting out thoughts of anger.

To eliminate obstacles to the far-reaching practice of joyous effort, abandon:

21. Gathering a circle of friends or disciples because of your desire for respect or profit.

22. Not dispelling the three types of laziness (sloth, attraction to distracting activities, and self-pity and discouragement).

23. With attachment, spending time idly talking and joking.

To eliminate obstacles to the far-reaching practice of meditative stabilization, abandon:

24. Not seeking the means to develop concentration, such as proper instructions and the right conditions necessary to do so. Not practicing the instructions once you have received them.

25. Not abandoning the five hindrances to meditative stabilization: sensual desire, malice, dullness and drowsiness, restlessness and regret, and doubt.

82   ASPIRING AND ENGAGING BODHICITTA

26. Seeing the good qualities of the taste of meditative stabilization and becoming attached to it.

To eliminate obstacles to the far-reaching practice of wisdom, abandon:

27. Abandoning the scriptures or paths of the Fundamental Vehicle as unnecessary for one following the Mahayana.

28. Exerting effort principally in another system of practice while neglecting the one you already have, the Mahayana.

29. Without a good reason, exerting effort to learn or practice the treatises of non-Buddhists which are not proper objects of your endeavor.

30. Beginning to favor and take delight in the treatises of non-Buddhists although studying them for a good reason.

31. Abandoning any part of the Mahayana by thinking it is uninteresting or unpleasant.

32. Praising yourself or belittling others because of pride, anger, and so on.

33. Not going to Dharma gatherings or teachings.

34. Despising your spiritual mentor or the meaning of the teachings and relying instead on their mere words; that is, if a teacher does not express him/herself well, not trying to understand the meaning of what he/she says, but criticizing.

ASPIRING AND ENGAGING BODHICITTA   83

To eliminate obstacles to the ethical conduct of benefiting others, abandon:

35. Not helping those who are in need.

36. Avoiding taking care of the sick.

37. Not alleviating the sufferings of others.

38. Not explaining what is proper conduct to those who are reckless.

39. Not benefiting in return those who have benefited you.

40. Not relieving the sorrow of others.

41. Not giving material possessions to those in need.

42. Not working for the welfare of your circle of friends, disciples, servants, etc.

43. Not acting in accordance with the wishes of others if doing so does not bring harm to yourself or others.

44. Not praising those with good qualities.

45. Not acting with whatever means are necessary according to the circumstances to stop someone from doing harmful actions.

46. Not using miraculous powers, if you possess them, to stop others from doing destructive actions.

Various Mantras

It is good to recite the following mantras in the morning to prepare for the day's activities.

Multiplying mantra

om sambhara sambhara bimana sara maha dzawa hung/ om mara mara bimana kara maha dzawa hung

The *Parinata-cakra-sutra* says that if this is recited seven times, whatever virtuous actions you do that day will be multiplied by 100,000.

Blessing the rosary

om rutsira mani prawa taya hum

In the *Palace of Vast Jewels*, it says to recite this seven times and then blow on the rosary to increase the power of subsequent recitations.

Blessing the feet

om kraytsara ghana hum hri soha

Reciting this three times and then spitting on the soles of your feet helps any living creature that dies beneath your feet that day to be reborn in the God Realm of the Thirty-three.

Blessing the speech

To the Three Jewels I go for refuge. May I become Buddha for the benefit of migrating beings. (3x)

I am the deity. On my tongue from an AH comes a moon disc. On it is a white OM. Around that are the white Sanskrit vowels standing clockwise. Around that are the red Sanskrit consonants standing anticlockwise. Around that are the blue syllables of the heart of dependent arising mantra, standing clockwise. Visualizing this, I recite these in succession, beginning with the innermost.

Sanskrit vowels: *om a a i i u u ri ri li li e ai o au am ah soha*[6] (3x)

Sanskrit consonants: *om ka kha ga gha nga/ cha chha ja jha nya/ tra thra dra dhra nra/ ta tha da dha na/ pa pha ba bha ma/ ya ra la wa/ sha shha sa ha ksha soha* (3x)

Heart of Dependent Arising: *om ye dharma haytu prabhava haytunte shan tatagato hyawadat/ teshan tsayo nirodha ewam wadi maha shramanaye soha* (3x)

(Phenomena arise from causes; those causes have been taught by the Tathagata, and their cessation, too, has been proclaimed by the Great Renunciate.)

Light from the OM and the mantra garlands summons inspiring powers of speech, worldly and supermundane, in the form of the three mantras, the seven perfect royal treasures,[7] and the eight auspicious signs[8]. These dissolve into the OM and the mantra garlands. Then the Heart of Dependent Arising mantra dissolves into the Sanskrit consonants, that into the Sanskrit vowels, that into the OM, and that into the moon disc. This transforms into an AH, which melts into white and red nectar and dissolves into the tongue, making it the nature of vajra.

The benefits of this practice are: the ability of one's speech is perfected, one's recitations are multiplied in strength ten million times; the power of one's mantra recitation is not diminished by eating black food (non-vegetarian food); one's idle talk becomes like recitation, and one does not accumulate so much negative karma from idle talk.

Eating meat

om ahbirakay tsara hung

Recite this seven times over the meat to stop the fault of eating meat and to help the sentient beings whose flesh it was to be reborn in a happy realm.

Mantras to increase merit

chomdenday deshin shegpa drachompa yangdakpar dzogpay sangye nampa nangdze okyi gyalpo la chag tsal lo (1x or 3x)

jagchub sempa sempa chenpo kuntu zangpo la chag tsal lo (1x or 3x)

tayata om pencha griwa ava bodhini soha, om duru duru jaya mukhe soha (7x)

chomdenday deshin shegpa drachompa yangdakpar dzogpay sangye ngowo dang monlam tamche rabtu drupay gyalpo la chag tsal lo (1x or 3x)

Scriptural Quotations for Meditation

Homages

I prostrate to the perfect Buddha,
The best of all teachers, who taught that
Whatever is dependently arisen is
Unceasing, unarisen,
Not annihilated, not permanent,
No coming, not going,
Without distinction, without identity,
And free from conceptual construction.

Nagarjuna, *Treatise on the Middle Way* (*Mulamadhyamakakarika*)

I prostrate to Gautama,
Who, through great compassion,
Taught the exalted Dharma
That leads to the relinquishing of all views.

Nagarjuna, *Treatise on the Middle Way*

I bow to the One Who Has Become Reliable, Intent on Benefiting
Migrating Beings, the Teacher, the One Gone to Bliss, the
Protector.

Dignaga, *Compendium of Reliable Cognition* (*Pramanasamuccaya*)

Beyond speech, thought, expression, wisdom gone beyond,
Unborn, unceasing, with a very nature like space,
Discerning transcendent wisdom's sphere of awareness,
Homage to the Mother of the three times' Buddhas.

Prajñaparamita Sutra

88   SCRIPTURAL QUOTATIONS FOR MEDITATION

By the knower of all, hearers seeking pacification are led to peace,
By the knower of paths, those benefiting migrating beings
accomplish the welfare of the world,
By the perfect possession of it, the subduers teach the varieties
possessing all aspects;
Homage to these mothers of the Buddhas, together with the host of
hearers and bodhisattvas.

> Maitreya, *Ornament of Clear Realizations* (*Abhisamayalamkara*)

The hearers and solitary realizers arise from the excellent sages
(Buddhas);
The excellent sages are born from bodhisattvas;
The compassionate mind and the non-dual awareness,
As well the awakening mind—these are the causes of bodhisattvas.

Compassion alone is seen as the seed
Of a Conqueror's rich harvest, as water that nourishes it,
And as the ripened fruit that is the source of long enjoyment;
Therefore, at the start I praise compassion.

Like a paddlewheel in motion, migrators have no autonomy;
First, with the thought "I," they cling to a self;
Then, with the thought "mine," they become attached to things;
I bow to this compassion that cares for migrators.

Homage to that compassion for migrators
Seen as evanescent and empty of inherent existence
Like the reflection of the moon in rippling water.

> Chandrakirti, "*Supplement to the Treatise on the Middle Way*"
> (*Madhyamakavatara*)

SCRIPTURAL QUOTATIONS FOR MEDITATION   89

Taming the Mind

Phenomena are preceded by the mind,
Ruled by the mind, made by the mind.
If you speak or act with a corrupted mind,
Suffering follows you like the wheel follows the foot of the ox.

Phenomena are preceded by the mind,
Ruled by the mind, made by the mind.
If you speak or act with a calm, bright heart,
Happiness follows you, like a shadow that never leaves.
    Buddha, *Dhammapada*

Attachment is no friend, but seems like one,
Which is why you do not fear it.
But shouldn't people particularly
Rid themselves of a harmful friend?
    Aryadeva, *The Four Hundred*

Just as a physician is not upset with
Someone who rages while possessed by a demon,
Subduers see afflictions as
The enemy, not the person who has them.
    Aryadeva, *The Four Hundred*

Do not commit any non-virtuous acts;
Cultivate virtues in as complete a way as possible;
Completely subdue one's mind;
This is the teaching of the Buddha.
    Buddha, *Dhammapada*

90   SCRIPTURAL QUOTATIONS FOR MEDITATION

Bodhicitta

Those who wish to crush the abundant miseries of conditioned existence,
Who wish to dispel the adversities of sentient beings
And who yearn to experience a myriad of joys
Should never forsake bodhicitta.

It is the supreme ambrosia
That overcomes the sovereignty of death,
It is the inexhaustible treasure
That eliminates all poverty in the world.

It is the supreme medicine
That quells the world's disease.
It is the tree that shelters all beings
Wandering and tired on the path of conditioned existence.

It is the universal bridge
That leads to freedom from unhappy states of birth,
It is the dawning moon of the mind
That dispels the torment of disturbing conceptions.

It is the great sun that finally removes
The misty ignorance of the world,
It is the quintessential butter
From the churning of the milk of Dharma.

Shantideva, *Guide to a Bodhisattva's Way of Life* (*Bodhicaryavatara*)

SCRIPTURAL QUOTATIONS FOR MEDITATION 91

Whatever joy there is in this world
All comes from desiring others to be happy,
And whatever suffering there is in this world,
All comes from desiring myself to be happy.

But what need is there to say much more?
The childish work for their own benefit,
The Buddhas work for the benefit of others.
Just look at the difference between them!

Shantideva, *Guide to a Bodhisattva's Way of Life* (*Bodhicaryavatara*)

And that which is dear to living beings
—hard to lose as their own lives—
May I hold that more dear than my own self.
May their bad deeds ripen upon me
And may all my virtue, without exception, ripen upon them.

Nagarjuna, *Precious Garland* (*Ratnavali*)

Devoid of all [substantive] entities,
Utterly discarding all objects and subjects,
Such as aggregates, elements, and sense-fields;
Due to sameness of selflessness of all phenomena,
One's mind is primordially unborn;
It is in the nature of emptiness.

Just as the blessed Buddhas and the great bodhisattvas have
generated bodhicitta, I too shall, from now until I arrive at the heart
of awakening, generate bodhicitta so that I may liberate those who
are not liberated, free those who are not free, relieve those who are
not relieved, and help thoroughly transcend sorrow those who have
not thoroughly transcended sorrow.

Guhyasamaja Root Tantra

When people see that joy and unhappiness are like a dream
And that beings degenerate due to the faults of afflictions,
Why would they strive for their own welfare,
Forsaking delight in the excellent deeds of altruism?
    Aryashura, *Compendium of the Perfections*

For as long as space endures
And for as long as living beings remain,
Until then may I, too, abide
To dispel the misery of the world.
    Shantideva, *Guide to a Bodhisattva's Way of Life* (*Bodhicaryavatara*)

Wisdom

"Self" is a demonic mind.
You have a wrong view.
These conditioned aggregates are empty;
There is no living being in them.

Just as one speaks of a cart
In dependence upon a collection of parts,
So we conventionally say "living being"
In dependence upon the aggregates.
    Bhikkhuni Vajira, *Samyutta Nikaya*

SCRIPTURAL QUOTATIONS FOR MEDITATION   93

Once there is self, there is other;
From this arise attachment and hatred to self and others
respectively,
So long as one is embroiled in these,
All faults will follow one.

> Dharmakirti, *Commentary on "Compendium of Valid Cognition"*
> (*Pramanavarttika*)

Through ceasing karma and afflictions there is nirvana.
Karma and afflictions come from conceptualizations.
These come from elaborations.
Elaborations cease by (or in) emptiness.

> Nagarjuna, *Treatise on the Middle Way*

Neither the aggregates, nor different from the aggregates,
The aggregates are not in him, nor is he in the aggregates.
The Tathagata does not possess the aggregates.
What is the Tathagata?

> Nagarjuna, *Treatise on the Middle Way*

As the tactile sense [pervades] the body
Confusion is present in them all.
By overcoming confusion one will also
Overcome all afflictions.

When dependent arising is seen
Confusion will not occur.
Thus every effort has been made here
To explain precisely this subject.

> Aryadeva, *The Four Hundred* (*Chatuhshatakashastrakarika*)

94   SCRIPTURAL QUOTATIONS FOR MEDITATION

A person is not earth, not water,
Not fire, not wind, not space,
Not consciousness, and not all of them.
What person is there other than these?

Just as a person is not real
Due to being a composite of six elements,
So each of the elements also
Is not real due to being a composite.

The aggregates are not the self, they are not in it,
It is not in them, without them it is not,
It is not mixed with the aggregates like fire and fuel.
Therefore how could the self exist?

Nagarjuna, Precious Garland

For one to whom emptiness makes sense,
Everything makes sense.
For one to whom emptiness does not make sense,
Nothing becomes sense.

That which is dependent arising.
Is explained to be emptiness.
That, being a dependent designation,
Is itself the middle way.

There does not exist anything
That is not dependently arisen.
Therefore there does not exist anything
That is not empty.

Nagarjuna, Treatise on the Middle Way

Notes

[1] "Lord Protector of Tushita's hundred gods" refers to Maitreya, the future Buddha. "Losang Dragpa" is Je Tsongkhapa's ordination name. His spiritual children are his two chief disciples, Gyalsabje, on his right, and Kedrupje, on his left.

[2] The meaning of this visualization is that the guru appears in the aspect of Je Tsongkhapa and is the Buddhas' wisdom, Manjushri. The guru appearing in the aspect of Gyalsabje is the Buddhas' compassion, Chenrezig. Appearing in the form of Kedrupje, the guru is the Buddhas' power, Vajrapani.

[3] The vajra symbolizes great bliss and the bell represents the wisdom realizing emptiness. Together, they signify his attainment of awakening, the inseparable unity of the truth body and the form body of a Buddha. Vajrasattva may also be depicted with his right hand holding a vajra at his heart and his left hand holding a bell in his lap.

[4] The five transcendental wisdoms are: mirror-like wisdom, equalizing wisdom, discriminating wisdom, all-accomplishing wisdom, wisdom of the sphere of reality.

[5] This explanation of the bodhisattva precepts is drawn from "Twenty Stanzas" by the Indian sage Chandragomin. He compiled the precepts from various sources: root precepts 1-4 and the forty-six auxiliary precepts are from the *Bodhisattva Bhumi* by Asanga; root precepts 5-17 are from the *Sutra of Akasagarbha*, and one precept is from the *Sutra of Skillful Means.*

[6] *i i* is pronounced *ee ee* (long *e* as in *beet*); *e* is pronounced as a long *a* as in *gate*; *ai* is also a long *a* as in *aisle.*

[7] The seven perfect royal treasures are the precious wheel, precious jewel, precious queen, precious minister, precious elephant, precious horse, and precious general.

[8] The eight auspicious signs are the right-turning conch, precious parasol, victory banner, golden fishes, Dharma wheel, endless knot, lotus, and great treasure vase.